Business (BAT Centre)

SID'S HEROES

SID JOYNSON &
ANDREW FORRESTER

BBC BOOKS

For dad

My first hero

This book is published to accompany the
television series *Sid's Heroes*
which was first broadcast in early 1995

Published by BBC Books,
a division of BBC Enterprises Limited,
Woodlands, 80 Wood Lane,
London, W12 0TT

First published 1995
Text © Sid Joynson and Lauderdale Productions 1995
Cartoons © Sid Joynson 1995
ISBN 0 563 37076 9
Designed by Casebourne Rose Design Associates
Illustrations by Sid Joynson
Set in Garamond
Printed and bound in Great Britain by Clays Ltd, St Ives plc
Cover printed by Lawrence Allen Ltd, Weston-super-Mare

CONTENTS

Acknowledgments

We would like to thank everyone who made this book possible, especially the companies concerned, the heroes who took part in the workshops and, where filming was involved, their families. We are also indebted to Peter Riding, at the BBC, who had the foresight to champion the series, and to Jonathan Drori, our BBC Executive Producer, for the valuable advice and support he gave us in making the programmes and, by so doing, indirectly contributing to the final shape of the book.

At Lauderdale Productions we want to register our appreciation of the efforts of the whole team. Brian Edwards helped develop the original concept, while Nicola Bungey, Sandra Hoggett, Jo Langford and Sasha Jeffrey played a key role in reading the proofs and checking factual accuracy.

Sid is grateful to all the previous heroes who have helped him develop the techniques illustrated in this book and the heroes in his own company, Jean, Sue and Sharon, who worked into the small hours of many mornings typing the revisions involved in creating the book. Without the support and forbearance of Suzanne Webber, Charlotte Lochhead, Esther Jagger and the rest of the team at BBC Books, this publication could never have emerged in its present unusual, and we hope stimulating, format.

Most of all we would like to thank our respective families. Both of us were lucky enough to have had the benefits of parents with good solid common-sense values derived from the communities of the industrial north of Britain. We have also been fortunate indeed to have had the support of our immediate families through the stressful schedule imposed by making a high-profile television series and writing a book at the same time. They have given us more understanding and sympathy than we sometimes deserved.

We reserve our warmest thanks to our personal heroes, Jean and Lis, our respective wives. They have inspired us more than they can ever know.

Sid Joynson Partnership is dedicated to supplying the tools and techniques that will help organizations achieve world-class levels of performance through the talents of their own heroes. Full details of the training workshops and materials can be obtained from the address below:

Sid Joynson Partnership, Alpha House, 2 Manor Park, Ledston, Nr Castleford, WF10 2BE, England
Tel: 01977 555304, Fax: 01977 604605

SOME INITIAL THOUGHTS

Before we start, I would like to say I am a helper of people, not an author. The excellence of the text is a tribute to Andrew Forrester my co-writer. I told the story and drew the pictures, but, having interviewed me at length, Andrew wrote the majority of the text (and produced the TV series). The object of this book is not to create a literary masterpiece, but to ask you to come on a journey with me to a new world, where I think you will be happier than you are in the one you live in now.

It is a world where we can compete internationally in manufacturing industries, and create the wealth we need to create a modern society where all our people can enjoy a good standard of living, and people of all ages and creeds will be treated with the respect they deserve, and feel a valued part of our society. The picture of this land will have to be built in your imagination, but once we have built it there, I will ask you to help build it in your physical world.

This book is a companion to the TV series *Sid's Heroes*, and if you have watched the programmes you will have seen groups of people starting on a journey of discovery and observed their experiences along the way. They started thinking they were just ordinary people, and ended up understanding that they were all heroes and could make a major contribution to the running of their companies. From the shop-floor to the board-room, there is a message here for everyone.

The only contribution I made was to convince the people involved that they were heroes (they were all the time, but just didn't know it), and provide them with various tools from my Taozen system to help them on their journey.

Enjoy your own journey.

PS One of the main tools we will require is our aerosol can marked 'Bullshit [BS] Repellent'. If you think anything in this book is BS you can spray Sid. You can also use the spray on all the BS in your private and working lives.

I hope that when you have finished reading this book, you will agree that all we really need is BCS (Basic Common Sense).

A LUCKY REMARK

by Andrew Forrester

> luck is simply the meeting of opportunity and someone prepared to seize it

In the fifties Japanese meant cheap and nasty – products that only the very poor or tasteless would care to buy. Japan's journey from joke to industrial giant has been put down to many things – a docile labour force, a powerful cultural tradition of loyalty to the organization, a clever industrial strategy pursued by Japanese governments, compliant banks, even an almost devilish refusal to let Western companies compete on fair terms. But these factors don't add up to a convincing explanation.

Yes, labour in that country seems contented and docile today, but in the 1950s Japan was racked by industrial unrest, with pitched battles being fought at factory gates between pickets and police. Where was the famed Japanese loyalty then? And why was the government in Tokyo able to pick winners so successfully when attempts to do it in Britain led to such fiascos as the Ryder Plan for British Leyland which planned for expansion that never came? It is hard even to argue that the advantage of cheap bank loans provided under the Japanese 'national plan' did any more than offset the extra burdens heaped on the Japanese economy by the oil price hikes of the 1970s. Unlike the USA and Britain, Japan had no fuel resources of its own. And if the Japanese have, it seems, stubbornly resisted the allure of Western consumer goods, that doesn't explain why we in the West overcame a strong post-war distaste for all things Japanese to fill our homes, our offices, even our roads, with products from Sony, Panasonic, Canon, Sharp and Nissan, all now household names.

In 1992, while researching a BBC *Business Matters* programme on why Japanese companies led the world, I telephoned a business contact.

'You should speak to Sid,' he said. 'Sid knows about Japan.'

Sid? The name had echoes of the cockney barrow boy, the wheeler-dealer. Maybe because in Britain a character called Sid had been the ingenious creation of an advertising team given the job of selling shares in British Gas, the formerly nationalized utility.

'Are you joking?' I asked.

'When you meet Sid you'll realize he's no joker. He's deadly serious and he makes deadly serious claims.'

'Such as?'

'Give him a workforce for two days and he'll raise productivity by 25 per cent – or your money back. Or cut waste by 50 per cent, whatever you prefer. And he'll do it without spending a penny.'

The claims were so extraordinary that I wanted to put them to the test. A week later we met in London.

Sid proved to be a curious mixture. He spoke in glowing terms about the 'heroes' he worked with – ordinary men and women who had always been treated as 'hands' by the bosses, but who could deliver the most amazing improvements in company performance in just two days. ('Actually, only one day,' said Sid. 'The first day of my workshops is usually spent getting the shit out of the system and giving the teams the improvement tools they will need.') Opposed to his heroes were the villains, some of the middle managers who could not or would not adapt to the new way, and who 'nobbled' his teams whenever they had a chance. 'When I find them,' he said, 'these are the bastards we have to crush.' Sid's use of such language, it proved, was not confined to private conversations. In his workshops it became a weapon to break down the barriers of suspicion – to great effect.

Although Sid occupied a niche within the broad spectrum generally referred to as 'management consultancy', he preferred not to use that term. 'I am a helper and facilitator. The people who do the business and come up with the improvements are the members of my teams. I make a point of knowing nothing about the companies before I go in, and when I leave I don't expect to be called back. The teams are the owners of the improvements, and once they understand the principle of continuous improvement they will go on finding better ways of working.'

I soon learned that Sid had strong feelings about the harm done by management consultants of the more conventional sort. 'They see themselves as experts bringing the benefit of their knowledge and experience to a company. In fact, very few of them have sufficient practical understanding of how a company works, and they place far too much faith in fancy theories and stuff they've read in books. That's what's wrong with Britain.' Sid's views on where British businesses were going wrong were equally uncompromising. Anyone who maintained that CBI stood for Complete Bloody Idiots was clearly not to be classed as mainstream. So I asked him where the rest of us were getting it wrong.

'By thinking that industrial expansion has to be led by investment,' said Sid. 'I've lost count of the number of times I've seen good money being poured into new technology before companies have cracked the question of how best the production flows should be organized. The new machines often only compound the problem. And new machines always beg the question: what do we do with the old ones we no longer need?'

'But that's not a question that arises,' I reacted. 'The old machines must be less efficient or clapped out. Bringing in new machinery and more modern technology must change things for the better.'

With a knowing look, all Sid would say, with that impish chortle that was his trademark, was: 'Does it indeed?' Casting his eyes around my library of business books he remarked that there was nothing more dangerous than the learned fool. 'You can read as many books as you like, but you will never truly understand until you do it. That is one of the fundamental lessons of Zen.'

Sid's approach, I was to discover, had a lot to do with the practical, common-sense values advocated by Zen Buddhism. So it came about that I learned to appreciate Sid's unique qualities as a facilitator. I took a train to Leeds to see him in action at a factory that was struggling to meet quality and delivery standards and was threatened by disaster if performance could not be dramatically improved. Sid was to run a two-day practical workshop.

The management had hired a team of consultants to improve matters, but it hadn't worked. After eight months of effort they had produced one big innovation – a gleaming new factory 'cell' designed to speed up production and cut down on waste and stocks. I found it manned by disgruntled workers who resented the new methods. Perhaps not surprisingly, the results had been disappointing. When they heard that a new 'consultant' was coming in, they told me, they regarded him as 'another bullshitter come to con the workforce'. Sid's target was to install two new manufacturing cells in two days and have them manned by an enthusiastic and happy workforce. It seemed a tall order.

At the morning session on Day One Sid was confronted by a deeply sceptical bunch of shop-floor workers (no managers are allowed to join these sessions) who were worried that his intervention would cost them their jobs. But by the mid-morning break he had begun to win them over. He did it by being stand-up comic, rabble-rouser and teller-of-home-truths in about equal measure.

'In this factory we have the managing director at one end and the bog cleaner at the other. Who do we miss first? Shit, isn't that a good question?'

Grudging laughter.

'Why does the night shift always work better than the day shift? Because we've got the managers off our back!'

Nods of agreement. More laughter.

'If we can't delight the customer by producing the highest quality, at the lowest cost, with the fastest delivery we're dead. Only world-class companies are going to survive.'

Zen, so Sid had told me, taught that when people were laughing they were more relaxed and open to learning. It certainly seemed to work here.

But it was the work of the teams that impressed me most. At first they showed some reluctance to embrace the idea that the true experts were themselves the people who did the job, not the 'smart-arses' who came in from outside with their university degrees and fancy qualifications. We had here battalions of people who had been led to believe from their schooldays that they were no good with their brains. Yet within a few hours they were assuming the roles of production planner and time and motion study expert – with startling effect. Production problems that had defied the expertise of their manager for months were solved with apparent ease. 'They don't have to think about it,' Sid told me. 'Zen means just do it.'

It wasn't merely the achievements that impressed. In just eight hours the attitude and appearance of the teams miraculously changed from sullen scepticism to confident enthusiasm. One of the workers in my team confided: 'I've really enjoyed myself.... I wouldn't have believed it possible, but we've done it.'

The rest of this book explores the philosophy behind Sid's unique method of changing attitudes within the workplace and of releasing the hidden talents that everyone has, even though they don't know it. Taking Sid into six companies chosen by the television research team, deliberately keeping Sid in the dark about the problems facing these companies, and then recording the outcome of his two-day workshops on camera, put his beliefs and his techniques to the most severe of tests. Readers will judge for themselves how well his ideas stood up.

My own view is that we *did* capture on camera some of the magic Sid finds inside the most apparently unexceptionable people. (In fact they were only seen as unexceptional because managements had never asked them to do exceptional things.)

What are the lessons of *Sid's Heroes* for Britain and the West?

Perhaps the most surprising question his work poses is whether we are fooling ourselves in thinking that investment in new machinery is the key to delivering higher productivity and better quality. If, as he claims, the average British factory operates at only 30 per cent effectiveness because of the inefficiency built into the system - too much waste, too much machinery down-time, too little capitalizing on the talents of the workforce - then enormous improvements in both productivity and quality can be achieved without any investment at all. Economists shudder when manufacturing growth exceeds 5 per cent per year - believing that it will lead to bottlenecks in supply and a rekindling of inflation. But Sid regularly demonstrates that any factory (even good ones) can increase productivity and quality, virtually overnight, by as much as 30 per cent, without spending a penny on new equipment.

Secondly, Sid's discovery that the secret of improved performance lies in using the 'real experts' - those who routinely do the job and who have acquired an intuitive understanding of the process - throws into question the conventional wisdom about the value of formal training *per se*. It certainly points to the need for less book-learning and for more on-the-job training through coaching, the transmission of skills through practice backed by the wisdom of experience.

Thirdly, *Sid's Heroes* raises fundamental questions about the workplace in Britain today. The latest IBM/London Business School survey of manufacturing companies found that only 2.3 per cent of British companies could be rated 'world-class'. 'World-class' almost by definition depends on having a committed workforce. Yet increased job insecurity, new 'flexible' shift patterns and the poor quality of too much British management, taken together, have made British workers the most stressed and unhappy in Europe.

Sid's message that we need to restore respect to people and give them a sense of security if we are to capitalize on talents of people, not only makes business sense, it could make Britain a happier place in which to live as well as work.

Andrew Forrester
SERIES PRODUCER
Sid's Heroes

CHAPTER ONE

A JOURNEY TO ENLIGHTENMENT

it is better to light
a candle than to curse
the darkness

In the 1960s the first Honda motorbikes appeared on the streets of Britain. If you are old enough to remember those days you may recall the open contempt displayed by the country's motorcycle enthusiasts (I know, I was one).

In Yorkshire they were dismissed as Fray Bentos motorbikes because we swore they were made out of used corned beef tins. They even had tassels decorating the handlebars. What sort of Yorkshireman would be seen dead on one of those? Real men didn't eat quiche and rode bikes that were – in our eyes anyway – the best in the world. Sitting astride a Norton or a Triumph you could attract admiring glances from the opposite sex and know that you could leave any Honda standing.

FRAY BENTOS HONDA

Thirty-five years on and everything has changed. Honda rules the world and Norton has shrunk to being a small specialist motorcycle manufacturer.

Sadly, the virtual death of the British motorbike has become the norm for many of our other manufacturing industries. Whatever became of British shipbuilding, machine tools and textiles? Sunk almost without trace. And our efforts to maintain even 'modern' industries such as cars, electronics and computers have not fared much better. Indeed, the fastest growing industry in Britain now seems to be the 'heritage' industry!

Between 1970 and 1994 Britain lost over 3 million jobs in manufacturing – jobs that have never been adequately replaced. The social consequences are there for all to see. As I drive round my native Leeds I see vast wastelands (often used as car parks) where there used to be factories; the new supermarkets and fast-food restaurants that have sprung up are no substitute for the creation of male unemployment. I am old-fashioned enough to believe that men find unemployment harder to bear than women, and young men hardest of all. And if we have failed to provide jobs for our young men can we really wonder why crime is soaring? People who have no stake in society take their revenge in the most anti-social ways.

It's fashionable these days to argue that advanced Western countries (a status that Britain holds on to by a whisker and could so easily lose) cannot compete in manufacturing terms with the emerging countries of the Far East. This view ignores two facts in Western economies, wages may amount to as little as 10 per cent of total industrial costs; and most factories, in my experience, operate at around only 30 per cent effectiveness (which means that the machinery is actually running for only about 30 per cent of the available time on a shift) and abound in what the Japanese call Muda – waste of materials, waste of time, waste of investment, in fact waste of every description.

The Japanese experience gives the lie to the notion that advanced countries cannot be manufacturing countries. Since 1970 manufacturing employment in Japan has actually increased even though wages and other costs have soared. Between 1992 and 1994 alone the Yen rose 30 per cent against the dollar, but the country's industries are well on the way to regaining a competitive edge. Even through the deepest recession that Japan has ever experienced, Toyota, for instance, has continued to be a very profitable company.

One key difference between Britain and Japan is that industrial leaders there accept responsibility for maintaining employment levels wherever they can. In Britain we give gongs to people who have destroyed jobs with the barbaric enthusiasm of Attila the Hun. Think about it.

It is time that we in the West sat down and considered the real lessons to be learnt from Japanese success. After the Second World War they had a bankrupt economy, and in the fifties a dreadful record on labour relations. Not even Arthur Scargill and his lads at Saltley Coke Depot could compete with the terrible clashes at the factory gates of some of Japan's biggest companies. But despite all this Japan in the sixties began to forge ahead, thanks to the work of men like Taiichi Ohno of Toyota Motors. Ohno and his like realized that the world was becoming an international marketplace and that the customer was king. It was their genius to devise a new way of working in the factory or office that delivered maximum customer satisfaction. Zero defects, just-in-time delivery, wide product variety – we have all heard the jargon, and many companies have tried to match the Japanese approach. However in seizing upon aspects of the Japanese way – Kanban, quality circles, teamwork – most companies have strangely neglected the underlying philosophy and the spirit that makes Japanese companies world-beaters.

Even when I made my first trips to Japan in the mid eighties I failed to understand what it was all about. I took with me my Western analytical approach and I tried to understand it intellectually, when what I really needed was to work with Japanese people and do the jobs they were doing in order to understand intuitively what made the factory hum. Why do Japanese companies make less use of computers? Why do they often use aging machinery rather than expensive new equipment? Why do managers spend more time walking about and less time in meetings? Why do they scorn such brilliant British inventions as BS5750? (The idiots, don't they know BS5750 delivers quality?)

It was only in 1990, after three more visits to Japan, that I really began to understand the Japanese way. I was working at Isuzu Motors with Yoshiki Iwata, a leading guru of Japanese manufacturing techniques, when the penny suddenly dropped. It was so simple that I scratched my head in wonderment that I had ignored the essence of the techniques for so long. And I brought back to Britain a determination to change my whole way of teaching - in future I would 'uncarve the block' and reveal the elegant simplicity of the method through a shared workshop experience with managers and with workforces.

It was never my intention to teach an unadulterated Japanese method of operation. The cultures are different and British workers are more independently minded than the Japanese, which I believe gives us an enormous advantage when it comes to improving the way we do things. Once you get a committed British workforce at your back you have an unstoppable momentum that can compete with any opposition. Sadly, so much of British management remains unaware of this huge untapped potential.

As we survey the British companies who took part in the search for 'Sid's heroes', I hope we will begin to see how that force can be marshalled and released, and how easily a wrong-headed management approach can nobble our heroes and return us to square one. The huge gains in productivity and quality, achieved without spending any money, are evidence enough of the effectiveness of the approach; it is time managers everywhere learned that lesson. Before we look at the companies, though, we must examine why the old way of working — the boss tells you to do something and you do it even if you think it's a crazy idea – is no longer appropriate as we face up to the twenty-first century.

In the nineteenth century all that mattered was price, and the classic British factory of a hundred years ago was very good at delivering low prices. But, as Japan has discovered, since 1960 customers have become increasingly sophisticated: they want good design, reliability, and above all choice, thrown in for free. The crisis of British mass production in the seventies should have told us that we needed to find better ways of working if we were to survive as an industrial power. Instead, our captains of industry opted for the easy strategy of closing down factories that were making losses. (I have always said that any fool can make a business profitable by closing down the loss-making parts; the real challenge is to take the loss-making activities and find a way of restoring them to profitability.) The result was a huge leap in British industrial productivity in 1981–2, hailed as a breakthrough by the CBI (which in my book stands for Complete Bloody Idiots), and a huge slump in manufacturing jobs.

At one point in the eighties our leaders seemed to take the view that manufacturing industry was a luxury that we could do without – what's happened to that idea now? A strong manufacturing base with responsive and effective companies serving a world market looks like a far better bet if our aim is to generate the wealth we need to maintain and improve our standard of living and – even more important – our quality of life.

I like to use the story of the road roller and the man walking in front to explain the relative decline of industrial Britain. The road roller is trundling along at 3 m.p.h., so what speed does the man have to reach to avoid being run over? Usually I get the answer: 4 m.p.h. or 5 m.p.h. It makes sense, but not for long. The man represents Norton motorbikes, best in the world, travelling at a steady pace and miles ahead of Honda in 1960. It is only when you fill in the detail that the road roller (Honda) is moving at 3 m.p.h.

OK?

3 mph   5 mph

but accelerating that the penny drops. If the man maintains his speed of 4 or even 5 m.p.h., the accelerating road roller will ultimately catch him up and flatten him. Too many British companies failed to perceive that *acceleration*, not *speed*, is the key. The successful companies are those which accelerate faster than their competitors.

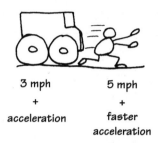

3 mph
+
acceleration

5 mph
+
faster
acceleration

But it would be wrong to relate speed and acceleration only to the volume of output. As we noted, customers too have travelled a long way since 1960. Nowadays they demand not simply a competitive price but reliability, choice and speed of delivery. In short, companies also have to deliver what customers want, when they want it.

The traditional factory coped adequately with the old-style customer who bought on price alone. But to meet the needs of the new consumer we must have systems that always deliver quality (zero defects), that can produce many different products out of a single factory (that was one secret of Toyota's success when it took on the US giants and won), and ensure speedy delivery.

Running this sort of enterprise (and it could equally be an office, warehouse or shop rather than a factory) requires a new approach. The old-style factory diminished people by employing them as mere 'hands' to do the job. In the new-style company, we need to employ people not as hands but as complete human beings, with *brains* that can be used to think, and *feelings* that can be harnessed for the good of the company.

The genuine world-class company, which is what I seek to create, is not divided down the middle by crude them-and-us antagonisms. Everybody should feel a genuine commitment to the long-term prosperity of the company, striving to maximize its total earning power and making sure that those earnings are divided fairly among the workforce, the management team and the shareholders. But while this seems almost self-evident, how many companies come within a million miles of the ideal? In the average company 20 per cent of its staff – the management team –

may appear strongly committed to seeing the company prosper, but even they are often at each other's throats. You don't find that sort of situation in big Japanese corporations. The Japanese learned some time ago that getting everyone committed and staying committed to the company objectives is fundamental to long-term success. We in the West, often driven by balance sheet madness, create companies where such commitment is rare.

There's a story told about a Glasgow shipyard that illustrates the point perfectly. In the early seventies a group of welders came up with an improved technique that meant better quality and increased productivity. They told the foreman, who passed the good news on to his manager. A week later the industrial engineers (and God help me, I used to be one of them) descended on the department and demanded two redundancies among the welders. Guess how many improvements the team came up with after that? And guess what did it do to morale?

That's why, before ever going into a firm, I make it a condition that no redundancies must result from any changes made through my workshop teams. Since the workshops produce massive savings in stockholding, reduce waste and result in a better quality product, companies are under no immediate pressure to reduce the workforce. In fact, at the Rawtenstall shoe factory (see Chapter 3) a stronger flow of orders actually offered the prospect of increased employment.

If we want to see everybody in the company all aboard the same boat and rowing in the same direction we have to change the rules by which we run that company. In the traditional factory there is a pyramid structure that places the MD at the top and the workers/staff at the bottom. This has to be replaced by an inverted pyramid (see diagram), with the customer, now at the top, being supported and delighted by a workforce who design and make the product or service just as the customer would like it to be. Beneath them are the managers who cannot satisfy the customer directly but can only do so indirectly by supporting the staff. At the bottom of the heap is the MD, who provides direction for the company but can only see

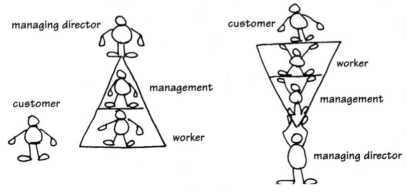

Traditional Factory **New Improved Factory**

his targets fulfilled by supporting his managers and above them his workforce. The inverted pyramid is not a new concept, but how many companies are doing more than play with the idea? In most companies I am afraid the cry remains: Managers Rule OK.

Getting commitment from the top (or – as we must now see it – the bottom) to this profound culture change within the company is vital. It requires a determination to remove any managers who stand in the way. But the good news is that, once we have this commitment, it is comparatively easy to make the change. Most business textbooks tell you that culture change can take up to five years to achieve. Unfortunately, by this time the business may no longer exist – there are world-class companies waiting to grab your customers. In fact a major change can be carried through in just two days, and the whole process should be completed in less than nine months! That's what this book, and the TV series, demonstrate. The key is to lead the workforce to change its perception of itself and the company through convincing them that *they* are the real experts and that *they* can deliver immense improvements more or less immediately, without spending anything. What's more, they can go on improving the operations year after year. They must be given ownership of the process and be supported in the changes they want to make. Even where mistakes are made, it has to be seen as part of the learning process.

Although this may sound like the pious mouthing of a theory-based management consultant, I want to stress that my approach is intensely practical. I never study the problems facing a company before I go in. Since I do not work for the company I cannot understand how it operates or what can be done to put the problems right: I leave that to the people who work there. Given the responsibility and a few simple tools, they invariably come up with solutions that leave not only me but also their own management 'gobsmacked'.

It may seem this approach is too simple but, believe me, it works. When I started out on the road I thought I was applying the Japanese principles of organization which themselves sat on a cultural underlay of Zen thinking and The Path of Tao. Only recently have I come to realize that the rudiments are founded not on some ancient Eastern philosophy but on something we had all along – common sense. We all have a store of traditional wisdom that has been shut out of our lives through our worship of the god 'Intellect'. Most of the principles I learned in Japan were taught me at my mother's knee and in my early days at Sunday school: necessity is the mother of invention; do unto others what you would have them do unto you; many hands make light work; and, most important of all, show respect to others. (It amuses my teams when I place the managing director at the top and the bog cleaner at the bottom of the company structure and ask the question: who do you miss first?)

My approach has two immediate benefits. The British educational system achieves what I call the 'no good' effect on the majority of those who pass through it: most people emerge from ten years of schooling with a very negative view of their own abilities. The dominant academic ideal appeals to some but disables the rest. Learning to wrestle with algebraic equations or to analyze Shakespeare's language pays dividends in opening the way to the professions and even to the board-room. But if these sorts of intellectual skills are beyond us, we soon get classed by the system as low achievers. Part of the transformation you see in any of my workshops comes from the realization that inability to prove Pythagoras's theorem doesn't mean you are stupid. In fact, everybody who does a job for any length of time acquires a completely different form of learning – intuitive learning, acquired  through doing by using all your senses. This is the first benefit of the Sid method. (For those of you who cling to the belief that intellectual training is by definition superior to intuitive training let me set a simple test: can you learn to play golf through reading a book?)

Secondly, the release of the workforce's intuitive skills not only raises morale – giving people a real sense of self-worth – but also produces solutions to everyday production problems that no amount of intellectual training can offer up. That is why it is crazy to leave managers, supervisors and technicians to make the decisions on how best to operate machines or lay out the workplace. They have a vital role to play instead, supporting these activities.

If we can learn to apply the simple Sid principles in business, there is no need to suppose that Britain cannot make up lost ground and become a great industrial power once again. After all, where was Japan thirty years ago?

Just when Japan was taking off as a world economy I was starting my own journey towards enlightenment. I was born in Armley in Leeds, a district of classic back-to-back terrace housing. People were not well off, but men had jobs and there was a real sense of community. Few locked their doors at night, and it was safe for children to play out on the streets or on the old slagheap left by a long defunct mine. My father, a native of Leeds, worked as a foreman in a tannery. My mother, who came from Shotts in Scotland, had arrived in Leeds in the thirties with her parents. Her father was an ex-miner who had lost his pit job after the General Strike of 1926 and found it difficult to get work up north. My mother, who is still alive, gave me a sense of values that have stayed with me all my life. She left school at fourteen and was by any standard poorly educated, but I now realize she possesses a natural wisdom gained from experience and I now apply many of her notions to my workshops.

School for me was a happy but wasteful experience. I failed my eleven plus examination and went to Crossgates Secondary Modern, a school reserved for the less academic child. I shone in no subject that carried any prestige. My one memento was the wooden stool I made (known in Yorkshire as a 'buffet') that I proudly took home and which still occupies an honoured place in my mother's living room. When I left school in 1956 it was assumed that I would get a factory job. Indeed, there were four or five possible jobs I could have taken – in stark contrast with the experience that most youngsters now face. I was accepted as an apprentice draughtsman in the West Yorkshire Foundries, then a flourishing company in central Leeds employing thousands of workers, now shrunk to a much smaller site and providing just three hundred jobs. Like another well-known British company, it is now owned by Germans!

Looking back on those days, I see that I had my first significant industrial learning experience there. As a draughtsman I had very little contact with factory floor workers. I would produce drawings for use on the shop-floor but I felt strangely out of touch. I didn't really understand how these parts fitted together, how they contributed to the whole. So after six months I applied for a temporary transfer to the factory. The idea of a draughtsman – who worked in an office and was a cut above the mere operatives who made the final product – taking a downward step to dirty his hands was greeted with astonishment, but I was given the chance I wanted. I understand now that the question of status within organizations is one of the most common obstacles to building a modern, efficient business. The closer you are to the customer, to producing the product or service, the less respect you get from management. These deeply stupid status systems have to be changed.

Working in the factory brought me face to face with everyday problems that we in the drawing office had no inkling of. Most people think that in a factory most of the time is spent making things, but in fact machinery can lie idle for much of the day. I discovered that machines designed to punch out a variety of metal parts had to be stopped and retooled between each job. Tool-setters would move in and change the dies – cutting tools made from hardened steel. This could take hours, depending on how complicated the operation was. I trained as a tool-setter myself, and it never occurred to me that this 'down-time' was costing the company a bomb and slowing up delivery to the customer. That was the way it had always been done.

My experience on the shop-floor earned me a chance to move back to the drawing office, this time as a designer. I had begun my progress up the ladder. Then, before I was twenty-one, I took my chance and moved to another big Leeds firm, Cameron Ironworks, to become an industrial engineer. There I set my sights on becoming works manager by the age of forty. I was clearly regarded as having management potential, because by the time I was twenty-four I had been recruited by another Leeds firm, Blakey's, to become a production engineer – a time and motion study man.

In the sixties it was all the rage to have 'experts' like me go round factory floors, timing operations and redesigning the layout. When I look back I blush at the arrogance I displayed as I walked among the operatives in my white coat, timing operations, having machines moved and drafting out new production schedules. They hated me, and to be honest I gave them a hard time (that's what management was all about, wasn't it?).

It was some years before I saw the error of my ways. I moved on to become part of a sales/demonstration team for one of Britain's top machine tool companies. I took the latest metal-cutting tools around factories and generally received a polite, even deferential welcome from buying departments. One day I called at a Sheffield factory and was shown to a workshop containing the biggest lathe I had ever seen. Unabashed, I selected one of our newest models and asked the operator to fit it to his machine.

The man, who was at least thirty years older than me, took one look at it and said: 'It's no good, lad.'

I was taken aback and irritated by what I took to be a typically Luddite attitude. It was the brainchild of the best designers in Britain, with degrees in engineering. 'We'll see,' I said as I deftly tightened the Allen bolts. 'Fire ahead,' I nodded.

The giant shaft began to turn and the cutting tool was gently brought to bear. Instantly there was a mighty crack and the tool splintered into a thousand pieces.

The operator looked at me as if to say: 'What did I tell you, you pillock!' Then he opened his toolbox, took out a cutting tool he had made himself in machine down-time, and passed it to me. 'Here, try this,' he said. It was a beautiful thing to feel and behold. More importantly, it cut through metal as if it were soft wood.

My encounter with Jim, who afterwards shared the secrets of his lathe with me, taught me that there was something wrong with our value system. People like him had a deep reservoir of knowledge based on practical experience, yet their views were ignored; worse, they were generally never even sought. But it was a reservoir that we ignored at our peril. Not that I immediately saw it that way, however. My initial reaction was to tap into the specialist skills of such people to improve my ability to sell tools; I never again fitted a completely unsuitable cutting tool to any demonstration machine.

I rose up and up until by the late 1970s I had become UK sales and marketing director of Carboloy, a company owned by General Electric of America – and I wasn't yet forty. But to be honest I wasn't really enjoying myself. I had been sucked up into a culture where to succeed you had to grind your heel into the faces of those below you on the ladder. You also had to watch your back because someone else was always after your job. It wasn't GE's fault – it was the prevailing culture everywhere.

Reaching the top echelon in a GE company had its rewards for those whose egos needed massaging. At one European sales conference held in Denmark, for instance, we were lavishly wined and dined and then entertained first by the Copenhagen Girls' Band and then by Victor Borge at the peak of his powers. It made you proud to be a GE man – but whether it improved business performance is another matter.

Whatever occasions like that did to ease the stress, it wasn't enough. I was spending less and less time at home. When I was there I was irritable and an uncomfortable person to share the house with. My wife Jean left me in no doubt of her feelings. With my three daughters lining up on her side, I felt it was time to make a break with the past. Much as I loved my job, I loved Jean and my children more.

So in 1982 I left Carboloy to set up my own company with Jean as my partner (I had met her when I worked in the office at Cameron Iron Works). She proved to have a natural business talent. Although I knew that the old ways of doing things were screwing me up along with countless thousands of others, I had no inkling that I was about to embark on my own personal road to Damascus. Jean and I spent a couple of years building up a common or garden sales training business, and then added training in people management techniques.

The years 1981–2 were boom ones for management consultancy. About a third of Britain's manufacturing companies went to the wall as interest rates soared and sterling shot up. Thousands of managers turned to consultancy and – with the new emphasis in Thatcher's Britain on giving managers the right to manage – there was a genuine interest in improving techniques. The trouble was that, in my experience, the proposed solutions didn't work. The consultants promoted one fad after another; each was embraced for a time by the management and then passed down to lower management to make what they could of it, which was generally very little.

This switching from one initiative to another every few years or months led to the creation of what I call the BOHICA effect. In seminars, when I ask my delegates if they have heard of her the answer is normally no. I then suggest that it sounds as though she might be Boudicca's sister or daughter – a young Celtic princess, driving round southern England cutting off the vital bits of Romans soldiers with the knives on her chariot wheels. I then go on to explain that it really means:

BEND
OVER
HERE
IT
COMES
AGAIN

Some time then has to be taken to explain that this programme is not another way of exploiting the workforce and BOHICA has no part to play in it. That is why, when I am called in by a firm, I encounter a wall of cynicism on the part of workers and even junior managers. They may never let the term cross their lips, but their faces speak more strongly than a thousand words – 'Bullshit, bullshit, bullshit.' And to be fair, with hindsight, some of the words that crossed my lips in my early workshops were very bullshitty indeed. But in 1986 came the flash of lightning.

I was working with a company in Doncaster, and the subject was Quality. I trained the sales force in delivering customer delight, I trained the managers in delivering quality products. But the products themselves remained mediocre and unreliable – no match for the Japanese equivalent. So I decided to invest the small reserve fund that Jean and I had in our company on a trip to study at the feet of the Japanese masters.

The most amazing thing I found about Japanese factories was the standard of cleanliness – you could eat your dinner off the factory floor. The second most amazing thing was the fact that the machinery was not particularly modern. Many of the machines I came across were ones I had worked on in the seventies. But the Japanese were producing three times as much per worker per shift. How was it done?

One reason was pretty obvious: they had laid out the machines in a way that enabled the products to flow through: there were no delays, no need to transport semi-finished articles from one workshop to another, no great piles of stock lying about. I remember thinking to myself that the production engineer who had worked this out must have been some sort of genius, and I asked who he was. I was shaken to the heels to be told that in Japan there was no equivalent of the British production engineer. 'The layout,' I was told, 'is the work of our workplace teams, who apply Kaizen techniques. That means they are continually improving the way we do things.'

I had read about Kaizen from a book by Shigeo Shingo, one of the team that developed the Toyota production system. Over the next two weeks I was able to see it in action, and I went back home determined to teach these techniques to British companies. But when they were translated halfway round the world they didn't have the same potency. I had analyzed the Japanese method and reduced it to a five-day seminar for managers, but although there was a fair amount of enthusiasm for the idea while they were on the course it didn't seem to last when they returned to work in their own businesses. It took another three years and four more trips to the Far East before I really began to understand what the Japanese approach was all about.

The first big revelation came when I went to work with a Japanese consultant called Chihiro Nakao. There were about a dozen Westerners on the project, which was based in a factory belonging to Isuzu Motors. We had been taught the principles of manufacturing cell design for one day and had taken copious notes, and now we were trying to design our own cell. We were all struggling with the paperwork, trying to figure out how best to lay out the machines, analyzing the problem and working out solutions in the time-honoured Western fashion, when Nakao came storming in and asked anyone who was ready to follow him on to the factory floor and start building the cell. Nobody stepped forward, much to the amusement of Nakao, who accused us of being 'Westerners with concrete heads'. This riled me so much that I stepped forward, armed with the rough sketch I had been working on, and told him to lead on.

The amazing thing was that, once I got on to the factory floor, the rough sketch was all I needed. I suddenly realized that you did not need a detailed drawing. It was much easier to work everything out by laying your hands on the machinery and physically moving it about. Although I did not appreciate it, I had learnt my first important lesson about Japanese techniques: don't agonize and think about possible solutions, just do it.

About two months later, browsing through some old books at a car boot sale, I came across a book on Buddhism, costing all of 25p, by a man called Christmas Humphries. One of the chapters, just twelve pages long, was on Zen Buddhism. When I read it, everything fell into place. The crucial passage ran something like this: 'In Zen we weary of study, we only wish to know.' And the only way we can know is to get out and do it. The book was screaming at me: 'To hell with all this analyzing – let's go out and do something!' Now I could go back to Japan and understand the processes. We must put aside our preference for intellectual learning – learning through the brain alone – and embrace learning through using all our senses: in other words intuitive learning.

But there was more to it than that. The Japanese had harnessed the power of three other concepts to drive their economy forward. The first was the power of the team.

In the successful Japanese company today everybody contributes to the fight against the competition. Everybody is pushing for improvement, and they are all pushing in the same direction.

In the average British company the situation is radically different. All the people are pushing, but not in the same direction. No wonder we don't seem to get as much done as the Japanese. It is hardly surprising that some of our people get tired of pushing and seeing nothing happen, and just stop trying. It is not enough to have the team trying hard. The team must be trying to go in

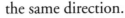
the same direction.

Teamwork brings great advantages. It pools the collective intuitive knowledge of the team members and can produce brilliant solutions to the most intractable of problems. It also builds strong motivation – far stronger than can be given by mere cash incentives. (In my experience, attempts to motivate through performance-related pay schemes are quite counter-productive and tend to destroy the all-important team ethic.)

Teams also allow us to tap into the awesome power that comes from group pride and peer group pressure. Take a group of twelve volunteer workmen on to Ilkley Moor and ask them to dig a hole twelve feet long, two feet across and six feet deep, using only small shovels. They will have to be prepared to stand in it all night, even though the weather forecast threatens heavy rain and sleet. It will get very cold and very muddy. Then at 4 a.m. they will have to walk six miles and do some strenuous physical work. Just for a laugh, before you set off tell them that there will be no overtime pay. Can you imagine what might happen? You're right – you're back in the hole by yourself and they're filling it in.

But let's transport them nine thousand miles away to the South Atlantic in 1982. Give them the extra challenge of two hundred enemy troops dug in at the end of their six mile walk, and tell them they'll be expected to capture the enemy positions. Lastly, give them a badge with a pair of wings and a motto: 'Who Dares Wins'. The rest is history.

The SAS won because they had a moral cause to fight for and a fierce pride in their 'company'. The Japanese company understands that fired-up people – committed to the cause, proud of their work – are the key to victory.

The importance of getting this sort of emotional commitment was recognized 2300 years ago by the Chinese general Sun T'su in his famous book *The Art of War*. He stressed that the first task of a leader was to create a moral cause for his people to fight for. I am sometimes alarmed that Western industrialists don't see business as a form of warfare. The casualties are not people's lives, but their jobs. As I pass through international airports in the Far East I notice that Sun T'su's book is still popular today among businessmen. Perhaps we in the West should read it too.

Just doing it, with teamwork and moral commitment, are two parts of the Japanese recipe for success. But any army also needs to be trained if it is to outperform the enemy. Here again, Western and Eastern approaches are quite different.

We tend to train highly, but in a single discipline. You might be a sales manager, for instance, or you might be a draughtsman. To gain experience and to develop your career you may move from company to company (I used to think like this, although I was lucky to have more than one skill). In Japan it is very different. There, it is the custom to stay within one company but to switch from job to job, which means that the workforce becomes multi-skilled. The best analogy is with the samurai warrior. He is armed with a bow and arrow to cut down enemies at a hundred yards, for slightly closer combat he has a spear, then a sword, and finally a dagger. If one weapon doesn't get you, another one will. Our managers and our workforces have to learn to be like this.

When I began my search for 'Sid's heroes' I set out to discover the real

champions in any company – the ones who are ready and willing to come to the aid of the business, provided we get them on the company's side. This book shows how to achieve that objective. The exploits I witnessed over the three months or so in which we filmed the BBC programmes were mind-boggling. Almost invariably we started with a suspicious, even hostile bunch of workers. After two days we saw them starting out on their journey. Our return visits three months later showed that this process, once begun, can develop a momentum of its own.

However, it is also a process that can so easily fall foul of unsupportive management – so one last lesson, then, from Sid's Guide-to-Beating-the-Japanese. Two and a half thousand years ago the Chinese philosophers distinguished between the two sides of human nature, Yang and Yin. Yang is the masculine side, represented by rock. It is tough and hard and bruising; it is also unyielding, and therefore brittle. Yin is the feminine side, which is represented by water. Water does not bruise but supports. Water is flexible and yielding. But water also finds a way round obstacles. When water and rock meet, it is the rock that eventually gets worn away.

The style of management that companies need today is one based on Yin rather than Yang. Managers were hard in the past, and in many companies it is the macho culture that still prevails. Under our new way of working the manager has to take the supportive role, to nurture people's talents, to encourage rather than criticize, to facilitate rather than command.

But, as we shall also find out, managers have to be tough too when the occasion demands it – usually when dealing with those at supervisory level who cannot come to terms with the new order. Remember that soft water, when frozen, turns to hard ice.

CHAPTER TWO

SHOWDOWN AT IPSWICH

help and protect the weak,
be equal to the strong,
crush the wicked

Samurai code!

Driving down from Leeds to Ipswich I had a premonition that Videoprint, a new company mass-producing video-cassettes for the British and European markets, was not going to be an easy nut to crack. Perhaps it was because the TV producer who had contacted the company and set up the filming had arched one eyebrow and said mysteriously: 'Sid, this could be a walk-out job.'

Making a television series about my work had seemed a good idea when it was suggested to me by Andrew Forrester at Lauderdale Productions, a company specializing in television business programmes. He believed that my message would catch the public imagination across Britain. But now, as the mileometer in the Peugeot estate ticked over on the M1, I was growing increasingly apprehensive. Could you capture real life on the TV camera? Or was it inevitable that the very presence of the camera and crew would distort the process? Would the magic I had helped to create in company after company across the UK melt away in the heat of the lights, making me look very foolish? But my biggest concern was that the process of making the programmes had meant passing responsibility for choosing companies to a TV production team, who could land me with a firm I would never have dreamt of working with.

Over the years I had developed a ritual, scrupulously observed, that had never let me down. It was a point of principle that I would not take on any work with a company unless certain preliminaries had been successfully negotiated. But with Videoprint this would not be possible – all I could do was conduct the final stage of this process, an interview with the MD which was just about to take place. But if he failed the interview, this time I did not have the option of withdrawing.

The full preliminary process normally goes like this. I get the initial message across to most companies at one of my public workshops on the principles of Building a World-class Company. Every year I run eight of these week-long workshops throughout Britain, and directors and managers come along usually on a word-of-mouth recommendation. After being exposed to the message the participants are fired up enough to take the idea of applying these principles back with them for discussion.

A few weeks after the workshop I often get asked to visit the company to meet the MD or chief executive. It is then that I sell them the idea that within the company there are heroes waiting for their talents to be released and that once these are released their achievements will be so awesome that any idea of going back to the old way of doing things will be unthinkable.

But to be honest, I don't go along merely to sell myself. If the process is to work I need to be sure that the man (or woman) at the top will take responsibility for driving the changes through. If that factor is not in place, there is generally no point in getting started. My message can be deeply unsettling to middle managers and supervisors, and many of them will resist change. But if they know I have the confidence and backing of their boss, they also know that if they obstruct the changes it will be at their peril.

I generally have a simple way of testing the waters. Do I see before me, in the boss's eye, a case of TLC or TDC? TLC stands for 'tender loving care': if the MD shows he cares for his workforce sufficiently to give them the chance to show what they can deliver, trusts them enough to let them take responsibility for improving their working methods, and respects them as fellow human beings, I have no qualms in tackling head-on the cynicism and hostility I usually meet when I first stand before the workforce. Regrettably, the chief executives or MDs willing to show even a modicum of TLC are, in my experience, not as common as we might wish.

Instead I often find TDC, an attitude that guarantees failure. It stands for 'thinly disguised contempt'. TDC often emerges when I talk of my notion of the self-managing workplace – a place where people have 'ownership' of the problems and the challenges, where supervisors don't snoop around 'checking up' on people, and people are not required to clock on and clock off. A common response from this kind of MD goes along the lines of: 'But Sid, it's not like that here. Give them an inch and they'll take a mile.'

At this point in the interview I stand up, politely excuse myself, pack up my case and leave... turning my back on thousands of pounds' worth of work. It is because I never compromise on this principle that I can stand up in front of workforces and tell them sincerely that I have the full backing of their top management.

So now, turning on to the A12 to drive the last few miles to Videoprint, in Ipswich, I tried to convince myself that the owner/chief executive of the company, Brian Bonner, was the sort of man I would not have walked out on. The research team had come back with widely differing verdicts. The researcher described him as a child of the Thatcher years, a bustling entrepreneur who had built this branch of the company up from scratch in just four years. But he was not closed to fresh thinking about making businesses better by ditching the notion that workers were a cost to the company and accepting that they could become its biggest asset. The producer, on the other hand, thought he was too self-centred and self-driven to have much concern for his staff; what mattered to him was his state-of-the-art factory and quality of product, which he thought depended largely on the technology. Brian Bonner was very proud that Videoprint was the largest independent video-cassette manufacturer in Britain.

I parked outside an anonymous-looking factory on an unnamed industrial estate. (It had to be anonymous to reduce the risk of organized robbery, the gateman told me.) The chilly feeling wasn't dispelled by the elaborate security procedure once I was inside. Everyone had to pass through a glass-sided passageway to reach the reception desk, behind which, for all to see, was the clocking-in and clocking-out area. The set-up did not exude a sense of trust. However, my initial reservations were removed in the course of the next half-hour. Brian Bonner was not at all pompous, and seemed to take a genuine pride in running a good ship. Without a hint of irony he told me that he liked to think it was a happy place in which to work.

I had worked in hi-tech factories like this before, but never on this particular product. One half of the factory consisted of a 'clean room', an area where staff had to wear special lint-free white overalls and hats. The other half consisted of the packaging and dispatch areas. Every day thousands of video-cassettes were packed into boxes here and dispatched to customers at very short notice. ('We have,' said Brian Bonner proudly, 'just-in-time delivery.')

It always amazes me how many British businessmen think they are doing things the Japanese way, using lean production methods, quality circles and so on. But it is a case of not being able to see the wood for the trees, seeing the part rather than the whole. I made a note that I would drive the point home during the workshop session – you must understand the philosophy behind the Japanese approach if you are to make the business hum.

The 'clean room' was obviously a source of great personal satisfaction to Brian Bonner. The machines were Japanese designed and built. The operation consisted of taking a master videotape of a feature film or TV series or pop video, and reproducing it at high speed on to individual video-cassettes. The basic raw material consisted of large rolls of virgin videotape wound round a central core. The large, flat reels were nicknamed 'pancakes', and the machines that did the transfer from master tape to the large reels were referred to as 'sprinters' – and by God did they go fast! In one day the factory could produce 75 000 cassettes. Brian Bonner explained that this was the best performance anywhere in the world. Although the Japanese had built the machinery, the layout and procedures had been developed here in the UK. 'The Japanese would not do it this way,' he assured me.

It was all very impressive on the surface. But I was struck by the fact that no member of staff seemed to know Brian Bonner and that he took very little interest in them. Did he unconsciously harbour the view that people are employed not as whole people but merely as 'hands' to do the job? And did he believe the ultimate aim was the automated factory without people? Fifteen years ago in Japan they shared that vision. But experience of automation has soured the dream.

The problem with robots is that they are stupid. They can be programmed to do tasks, but as soon as anything unexpected happens they are all at sea. Modern factories and offices need to be manned by thinking, caring people who can solve problems as they arrive and come up with better ways of doing things. That is why companies like Sony which in the past put together total automation packages have modified the idea. Experience with computers and automation has reinforced the Japanese view that simple, human-scale manufacturing control systems are really what matters. Businesses in the West, Brian Bonner's among them, still have to learn that lesson.

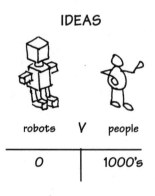

IDEAS

robots V people

0 | 1000's

Yet, sitting in his office after our tour of the works, I was inclined to give him the benefit of the doubt. He genuinely believed his production system would be very hard to improve on, and he obviously saw my proposal to take a group of twenty-four workers – some from each part of the factory – and set them free to improve the place as a challenge to himself. It was a challenge that I was happy to hand over to his workforce. No group of workers had ever let me down in the past, and I was sure (and still am) these Suffolk folk would be no exception.

The filming had gone well, and everything seemed set for the return visit, when Brian Bonner made the sort of unsettling comment that should have set the alarm bells ringing. I was explaining how my heroes would come up with better ways of running the factory when he let slip the basis of his personal doubt.

'We have supervisors here,' he said, 'whose job it is to find better ways of doing things. So they are doing the job already.'

'Oh, no,' I countered, 'the people who do the job will come up with much better ideas than your supervisors. They are the real experts – they understand the processes.'

'Experts, yes,' replied Brian Bonner, 'but only at what they are doing. They cannot take a wider view.'

I explained that, once you took these 'experts' throughout the factory and put them together as a team, they would be able to do just that. But I still felt uneasy about his assumptions. Whether he turned out to be the sort of chief executive I would walk out on, only time would tell.

The next step was the *Sid's Heroes* management conference in a Manchester hotel. We had invited all the companies taking part in the TV series to send three management representatives on a crash course in the art of Zen applied to the workplace. Since managers are entrusted with carrying on the process after my practical workshop sessions with the workforce, it makes sense for those managers to understand what we are trying to achieve.

As the groups settled down, I scanned the room for Brian Bonner. He wasn't there. Lee Paterson, the Videoprint works manager, and Simon Valley, the group manufacturing director, introduced themselves. They apologized for his non-appearance, explaining that he had had to go to France on urgent business. Thus it was that Brian Bonner would come along to the workshop session later without a proper grasp of the process and the thinking behind it. The seeds of potential disaster were sown.

I met up with the television crew late on a summer's evening outside the Videoprint factory. Some time had passed since the Manchester conference, and they had been back to Ipswich to film some of the workers at home with their families or out with their friends. This was the result of a remark I had made to Andrew Forrester when we were discussing the making of the TV series a year earlier. I had told him I was always amazed at how much energy people throw into their lives outside work. If companies could only channel some of that energy and enthusiasm into the business, think what strength it would give them! Yet very few companies manage it.

The crew had filmed some of that energy and enthusiasm to great effect. Dawn Webster and Sarah Pothecary, who worked in the 'clean room', were found to be keen horse-riders. Dave Lee, a tall black lad with a strong personality who worked in the packing area, had a secret ambition to lead his own professional ragga band. David Richman, who inspected videos as they came off the production line, was perhaps the most interesting of all. He lived in a caravan with his partner and daughter and was a keen amateur video maker – not the family holiday or wedding type stuff, but real little dramas. He had shown the crew his version of a popular thriller in which his wife played an alien who had come to destroy the world. One of the highlights was the ending, when she was disposed of by being pushed over a cliff. She upended herself in a most dramatic way before disappearing down a slope. 'I suddenly thought – God, she's pregnant!'

Dave told the crew. 'But I couldn't just drop the camera and run to help her.' As it happened, no harm was done.

Interesting though the television people found this sort of human interest material, the most important part of the filming was when they asked each employee what they thought of the firm and of someone called Sid coming to shake the place up. Although I know now the hatred they had for the company, I had no inkling of this as I set up the hall for the two-day workshop. It was large and generously endowed with tables and chairs, and lunch had been laid on for both days in an adjacent room. Videoprint seemed to have come up trumps.

DAY ONE

I fingered my pointer nervously as the twenty-odd volunteers for the course slid into their seats at eight o'clock sharp. They looked a good bunch, split roughly half men and half women. On occasions like these I know I am always going to have a tough time, certainly for the first couple of hours. Sticking a label marked 'Sid' on my shirt, and passing round the labels for everybody else to name themselves, helps to break the ice. But at Videoprint there remained an undercurrent of suspicion, an air of cold cynicism.

My techniques have been honed with time and experience. I am one-third stand-up comic, one-third teacher and one-third passionate champion of the hero that resides inside everyone. Laughter not only puts people in a good frame of mind, it allows them to take in uncomfortable truths: the Zen masters had long ago recognized that. The 'Bullshit Repellent' can which I always bring with me, is a good example. Anyone in the room is free to use it, including me, and it makes a point while also raising a laugh. Add to that a stock of funny stories, and I usually get down to the nitty-gritty remarkably quickly.

I begin with the new world we live in. Competition is fierce, and only the best will survive. We can do this only by continual improvement and faster acceleration than our rivals. To achieve that we have to use the talents of the experts (BOHICA usually threatens to mount her chariot at this point): 'The experts are the key to success, but not the smart-arsed experts who are used to operating from an office and come down and tell you what to do. Oh no – I mean the real experts, you.' At Videoprint, as at most companies I go into, this last statement was met by a laugh – of disbelief.

And my next revelation almost brought the walls tumbling down because it seemed even more far-fetched. The real experts would work together in teams to achieve four things. They would make the job easier, faster, safer and (wait for it) fun. It is always hard for workforces to buy into that idea. Making the job faster is what managers have been trying to do for years. It is what the old time and motion study was all about. I used to do that myself, and I know now how unfair it was to the workers. We would descend from on high and ask them to go through a cycle of work which we timed to the second. Then we made an allowance for the fact that the bastards were going slow for our benefit, and drew up the production schedule. (Unfortunately we were more concerned with units of production than with quality of output.) Under this old way of doing things, making the job faster meant working harder and possibly cutting corners on safety. Certainly it was never fun. Can we blame workers for kicking against such management initiatives? But now what I suggest is a completely different approach, in which making the job fun is the most important first step.

Jobs can be made fun in a number of ways, but the most important element springs from job satisfaction. In a factory environment where jobs may seem repetitive and boring that might seem a tall order. In fact it is easy to achieve. Firstly, we need a sense of emotional commitment to the job. That is done by making everyone aware that, whatever job they have, it is very important. And this is not bullshit. Unless a company is very badly run everybody's job is important, although it may never have been pointed out to the person doing it.

Take the example of a bricklayer who works day after day placing brick upon brick on a featureless wall. Who could blame him for feeling emotionally detached from the job? But if he is involved enough with the project overall he would know that he is building not a wall but a new operating theatre in a hospital, and that he is part of an enterprise that will save lives and give new hope to relatives and friends. This of course is an extreme example, chosen to make the point. But the principle generally applies: if businesses involve people, set goals that can be shared by everyone in the company no matter what their job is, and make people feel that their job is vital to the success of the whole enterprise, then those businesses will be handsomely repaid in loyalty and commitment.

wall

hospital

But there is more to job satisfaction than knowing you are important and respected for the job you do. You also have to feel you have control over your working life. This means that managers have to learn to stop telling people what to do and instead pass responsibility for reaching goals to the workforce. This sort of advice has become business orthodoxy all over the Western world, but in my experience very few companies do more than pay lip-service to the idea. The gulf between stated intention and the actual outcome is immediately obvious to someone in my position – someone who listens to managers boasting of their latest achievements in 'empowerment' and then discovers how little of it there is in practice. (The cynicism with which Mission Statements are greeted on the shop-floor is a reflection of how far apart theory and practice have drifted.)

There's a third magic ingredient in any recipe for making work fun – the team. Again it can be demonstrated through the workshop approach. We rescue individuals from their islands of isolation in the workplace and create teams of people who tackle jobs together. So long as we work only as individuals we cut ourselves off from the uplifting sense of all being in it together, of being able to bring collective experience to bear to solve problems, and of sharing the humour that comes from social interaction.

My workshops are always fun. But that was not how things were developing at Videoprint.

'You see, man,' said Dave Lee. 'It has got to work both ways. We don't think the management here can change. We can come up with ideas of how to make the place run better, but they won't listen to us.' There was a general murmur of agreement.

After coffee at ten o'clock the film crew left me to get on with the routine part of the course. As soon as I walked back into the conference room I felt the growing tension. Freed from the restraints of being on television, the workshop volunteers laid their cards on the table.

The greatest beef concerned the hours of work. The factory worked forty-four hours a week – above the national average. However, what made this such a strain was the practice of working twelve-hour shifts – four days on and four days off, day shift and night shift alternating.

'It plays hell with your body clock.... We walk about like zombies for half the time.... And we're often asked to work overtime when there's an absentee on the incoming shift... We never know whether or not we can have Christmas off until the very last moment.... We only do it for the money.... If there were other jobs available we wouldn't be here.... We hate our work.'

I was quite taken aback. Never in ten years of running workshops had I come across such an outpouring of hate and despair. Even if I could win the confidence of this workforce, could I turn them into heroes? My usual line is to argue that I couldn't change the past but we could begin to build a new future here and now. When the teams produced their results on Day Two their managers would have to be idiots to turn the clock back.

'You don't understand,' said Dave Lee. 'The managers may be impressed, but it won't mean a thing if Brian Bonner says he wants things to stay as they are.'

'And Brian Bonner won't change,' said another.

I was up against it. I reminded everybody that I had come with cast-iron assurances that there would be no redundancies and no recriminations, and that the company must be serious about finding new ways of working or they would never have allowed the TV cameras in. But none of these arguments made any impression. So there was nothing for it but to suspend the workshop while I went to speak to works manager Lee Paterson in his office. I was totally frank. I told him we had a crisis on our hands since the workforce were not convinced that Brian Bonner and the rest of the management would back them. Unless he came along to persuade the workers that this would not be the case, the whole project would have to be abandoned.

Lee rose to the occasion. Dropping whatever he was doing to come and address the workers was clearly an uncomfortable experience. Macho management dictates that managers should never look weak in front of the troops, and I guessed that at Videoprint macho might be seen as the norm. Yet he came over with me, asked to be left alone with the workshop teams and spent half an hour locked in discussion. He emerged looking flustered and hot under the collar, but announced: 'They've decided to carry on.'

What Lee had said to them, what guarantees – if any – he had given, I do not know. But the very fact that the manager had descended from on high to speak to them had made an impression. They looked to me for the first step. 'I want to begin,' I said, 'with Jean's kitchen.'

From then on the Videoprint workshop went very much as all my workshops go. Although we had seen worker disaffection here on a grand scale, most workshops can only settle down to the job in hand after getting the accumulated resentments of years of exploitation out of the system. After Lee Paterson's intervention the team were at least willing to have a go. But we were now two or three hours behind schedule, and I needed real commitment if we were to get the show back on the road.

I started with Jean's kitchen as the fastest way of getting across the message that an efficient workplace needs to be a tidy workplace. Some people feel it is sexist to use my parable of the kitchen to get the message across. Why should the person in the kitchen be a woman? Well, in my household it happens to be the way things are, since I spend much of my time away from home and inevitably Jean sees the kitchen as hers. As my business/life partner Jean also runs the internal administration of our business. But I chose to put the woman in charge of the kitchen in my story for another reason, too: in my experience, women have an intuitive understanding of workplace efficiency – they possess more Yin than Yang. So in my story Jean has the kitchen and I have the garage.

As I describe it, my garage is 'interesting'. I have drawers into which I cram my tools, I have a workbench piled high with the remnants of my last job, and I have a six-inch gap between the bench and the wall so that I can sweep the rubbish down the back. And, not surprisingly, I have an interesting collection of bits and pieces under the bench: clapped out batteries, some bits of wire, an old headlight reflector, even a set of imperial-size tools. Everyone knows the scenario. I keep all these bits and pieces 'because I never know when I might need them'. The problem is that I can never find anything when I really want to, and the place gets ever more cluttered because my grandchildren play in it and seem to think it is fine to drop their sweet papers and leave a few old and broken toys lying about.

This is something they would never do in Jean's kitchen. It is kept

kitchen

garage

spick and span, there's a place for everything and everything is in its place; because it looks like that, no one drops their rubbish in it – or if they do it is immediately spotted and removed. As a result, when Jean sets to work she can always find whatever she needs.

Now my garage stands for the average British factory, Jean's kitchen for the Japanese factory. Guess which one is more pleasant to work in? And which is the more productive?

'How would you rate the "clean room" here at Videoprint?' I asked the team who worked there. 'On a scale from good kitchen through to bad garage, would it be a less-than-perfect kitchen?'

Surprisingly, they rated it as a bad garage.

With the afternoon racing away we buckled down to acquiring the skills they would need to analyze where things could be improved in the factory. The basic skill package on this workshop is called TPM – Total Productive Maintenance. The word 'maintenance' is used here not just in connection with the machinery, but also in relation to the performance of the factory in the long term.

The goals of the programme are to reduce to zero the four Ds:
- Down-time
- Defects
- Delays
- Damage to people

To do this we use three techniques:
- 5 S Housekeeping – the Japanese approach to organizing workplaces.
- CID Chart – meaning Continuous Improvement Diagram. This is a system which enables you to analyze problems and create action plans to implement their solutions.
- SOP – meaning Standard Operating Procedure. How to create a standard procedure that will produce the same product whoever is using it.

These techniques are relatively simple (see page 180-187) and rely on tapping into everybody's intuitive skills, pooling the resources of the team, generating fresh ideas and putting them to the test – and I marvel that we ignored the potential of this process for so long.

By five o'clock the Videoprint teams and I had decided that next morning we would undertake four projects to prove how effective the new approach was.

But I still had my doubts about whether the magic would work. In my hotel room that night I tossed and turned. I could still hear the voices. 'They won't listen... they won't listen... they won't listen.' I wondered just what Brian Bonner was going to make of it.

DAY TWO

There seemed to be a better spirit the following morning. People appeared fresher. Most of the people on the course had just come off night shift, and perhaps that had fuelled a lot of yesterday's bitterness; only time would tell. Certainly by nine o'clock the four project teams were fully engrossed in the tasks they had set themselves.

The biggest group had decided they wanted to transform the 'clean room' from a bad garage into a good kitchen. They set off to analyze where the procedures could be improved, keeping a keen eye open for the chief villain, Muda.

The second group applied themselves to the task of redesigning the packing area, using a technique first developed in Japan to create efficient cellular manufacture. Within a few minutes they were out on the shop-floor timing operations with a stopwatch – showing that, in the hands of a team of workers firmly focused on achieving a business goal, the stopwatch becomes a mighty tool, not an occasion for a walk-out. They set about 'walking the job' to establish how much time represented avoidable waste.

The third group gave themselves the goal of preparing a training manual for operators on the 'sprinter' machines. It was to be easy to use, written in everyday English, and matched to photographs and diagrams wherever possible.

The last and smallest group set themselves the task of reducing the time needed to change over machines from one mode of production to another.

It was important that all the groups chose for themselves what they wished to tackle. Ownership of the process clearly lay with them. To reinforce the message, as they set off on their mission to improve, I did what I always do in my workshops at this stage – I deliberately stayed behind in the conference room.

It is on the second day that the magic really happens. The cynicism of Day One seems to evaporate through the sheer exhilaration of being in charge, working together to come up with solutions, proving that the new ideas can work. If there is a drug that produces the magical effect of smiling faces among the workers, and dramatic changes in hours rather than days, it is the drug of growing self-belief, manufactured by the powerful insight that they, as the real 'experts', are the people who count. In my experience, one afternoon of team problem solving creates more good ideas than a year of 'suggestion' rewards.

When, just an hour later, I made my way suitably togged up into the 'clean room', it was hard to recognize the embittered people I had faced just twenty-four hours before. Unnecessary equipment, tools and stock had been moved away, a place for storing the tools that were actually needed had been designed and laid out, and a dangerously top-heavy machine modified to make it safe. Dawn summed it up. 'We've been trying to get something done about that machine for months,' she said. 'Now we're putting matters right.'

Then I went through to the packing area, to find tables being rearranged and the flow of work changed to make it easier for the packers. Dave Lee, armed with stopwatch and carrying his tall frame with almost a swagger, announced that they had set a target to speed up the process by 20 per cent through making the job easier and cutting out waste. 'Our aim is to show that our method works better than the one we've been following up to now.'

Armed with a Polaroid camera to take pictures of what actually happened, the training manual team had broken the instructions down into a few easy-to-follow steps. 'Now, when temporary staff come in – and we have a lot of them when the pressure's on – we'll be able to train them in half the time,' said Perri Green, one of the team.

Only the fourth group seemed to be struggling. Their idea was not working out. 'Come back to the conference room,' I said, 'and let's work out how to fix it.'

By four o'clock the teams were back. Their reports had been written up, and their suggestions on how to make sure the business would go on improving in the years to come had been spelt out on flip-chart boards. To the question on how the business could be improved most easily, they had all given the same answer: by putting an end to 'them and us' and having managers and workers working together. In the light of what was about to happen, another question brought forth a prophetic answer. Asked what could prevent the necessary changes taking place, every team had replied: managers and workers not listening to each other.

As we sat and waited for Brian Bonner and the managers to arrive for the presentation in the conference room, I reflected on the fact that I had never yet come across a workforce which would not buy into my vision of a factory or office where everyone treated others with respect and where people were encouraged to make a bigger contribution to the success of the company. If workforces are willing to bury the hatchet and let bygones be bygones, it is up to managements to make the effort to bridge the gap. If you were to ask me whether managers should be willing to go halfway to meet the workers in building new relationships built on trust and respect, I would reply that they must be prepared to go much more than halfway. Too many workers have been abused by macho styles of management for managers to expect them to have faith in the new relationship at the first hand of friendship or the first word of encouragement. In fact, the further managers go towards treating their staff as their equals as human beings, the more dramatic can be the rewards. Symbolic gestures can be particularly important in sending the message: things are going to be different from now on.

As Brian Bonner and his managers strode purposefully into the room at five past four it was hard to read their intentions from their faces. All the managers, from Simon Valley down – about eight in all – were dressed in neat short-sleeved shirts and brightly coloured ties, a trendy sort of corporate uniform. Brian Bonner himself was dressed more casually in a polo-necked shirt and sports jacket.

I gave them a little speech of welcome and asked them to take up position along the back of the room where they could see the presentations. This is normal procedure in my workshops and I have never found a management team that had to think twice about it. Not, that is, until now.

'How long will it take?' asked Brian Bonner. I told him I estimated between fifteen minutes and half an hour. 'In that case,' he said, 'we'd prefer to sit.'

The proceedings were held up while the seating was reorganized but, once done, the managers and workers were seated cheek-by-jowl and at the same level. If anything, this could help break down barriers and encourage informal discussion.

Dawn spoke first, on the clean-up operation in the manufacturing area. 'We set out to change it from a bad garage to a good kitchen. We started by labelling everything in the area that wasn't needed, and removed it. We created shadow boards where we could hang up the tools we need. If anyone uses one they'll return it to its proper place.... If they don't, we'll pretty soon see it's missing.' At this point she looked with light-hearted menace at her fellow team members before going on: 'After that we cleaned the room up and created a work area that people would be proud to work in.' I had a mental picture of Dawn grooming her machine with the same care and pride she showed to her pony. She went on: 'At the end of each shift the aim will be to leave the workplace in the state it was in to start with....'

I noticed several of the managers scribbling away like fury as they listened to Dawn's explanation of how things should be in future. That might be an indication that the points were being taken seriously.

'Provided we all stick to the plan,' she concluded, 'we'll cut out a lot of wasted time looking for things and generally we'll all be a lot happier.'

Dawn sat down to clapping from the work-teams and a trickle of applause from the management team. By this time I had noticed that they all seemed to take their lead from Brian Bonner.

She was followed by Dave Lee, who gave a virtuoso performance in reporting on the packing exercise. 'Our aim was to show managers that if they listened to us and did it the way we think is best there would a big improvement. We worked out a better flow of work, with less time being wasted walking back and forward... we timed it over 200 units using the old system first and then using our system. We have improved productivity by 20 per cent and saved the company a lot of money....'

I particularly liked Dave Lee's stress on how much money could be saved rather than spent. I thought that would go down well with Brian Bonner who I knew cared very much for his bottom line.

Then came Perri with the training manual project. This time there was a decided wit about the presentation. She and her team knew how the 'sprinters' worked from operating them, rather than from reading the manual, which was a massive and indigestible document. Come to think of it, most manuals share these characteristics: trying to write down the procedures in totally unambiguous terms seems to require such a lot of words, and even then they are not clear. Using photographs, with text spelling out steps 1 to 10, looked much clearer.

```
tall dark
handsome
5' 10"
14 stone
glasses
blue trousers
```

The winding up came with Perri reading out a typical instruction from the old manual 'The remaining number of pieces is nought'. With a smile she read the new version: 'Pancake has finished sprinting, switch the machine off', and sat down to warm applause.

I rose with a naive confidence, using a tone of voice that suggested: Beat that if you can! 'Well,' I began, 'what do you think of that?'

A moment's silence. The managers looked to Brian Bonner to say something first. Without rising, he uttered the memorable words: 'I expected a bit more.'

My jaw dropped visibly , as I discovered later when I watched the TV programme. It was the last answer I had expected. Before I could say a word, a good half-dozen workers stood up and walked out.

'What do you mean?' I was still searching for words.

'Well, I was hoping there would be some more ideas orientated to improving productivity or efficiency.'

'But Dave Lee told us they had improved the flow in the packing area by 20 per cent and the changes that Dawn's team wants to make will speed up production – less time lost, everything where it should be. That will produce productivity improvements, won't it? Or am I seeing things all wrong?'

Now that Brian Bonner had spoken it had opened the floodgates, and the managers piled in behind him to try and disprove the idea that there would be any benefits. Terry Scott, the shift manager in the 'clean room', decided to have a go at Dawn personally.

'Dawn is the shift leader, and it's her job already to keep the place clean and tidy. So what she's doing is criticizing herself.'

Dawn struggled to hold back the tears as she protested that it was not good enough to try and blame her: she inherited the room from other shifts... everyone had to change... at least they had made a start.... In the most poignant reversal of roles she told the managers: 'We really care about this place. All we want to do is to be allowed to make it better.'

Other managers now joined in, questioning Dave Lee's figures and saying: 'We tried it Dave's way and it didn't work.'

I suddenly realized that instead of supporting the workers and encouraging them, the managers were competing with them: they had failed to grasp that the whole purpose of the exercise was to tap into the expert knowledge of the operatives, and that all the ideas would have to be tested before they were implemented – but tested by the operatives themselves, not by the managers. What we were seeing today was only the start of a long process. Debating whether or not these ideas would work was falling back on the Western love of abstract analysis, and was stopping things happening.

'Do you see what you're doing to them?' Now I had got angry. I turned to Brian Bonner: 'In two minutes you've bleeding destroyed what has taken two days to build up. They told me you wouldn't support them, and they were right.' Addressing myself to the workers now, I said: 'I owe you a sincere apology.' Then I asked Brian Bonner why he had spoken as he did.

'Because that's what I felt, you big prat,' he replied.

Since I am of less-than-average stature the remark seems funny in retrospect but at the time it didn't register. All I could feel was the hurt and anger of the heroes.

I turned and walked out, leaving behind a heated argument between managers and workers. Almost the last snatch I heard was Dave Lee's voice

raised excitedly: 'But Brian, we're not Sid's heroes, we're your heroes.'

As I packed up the car to leave, I let my thoughts flow to the camera: 'And now we wonder why we can start up manufacturing industries but we can't sustain them. These people are the bedrock of any company. Without them a business is built on sand. With your people on your side you can build a business that will last forever. Without them, God help us. I am very, very disappointed, and very sad.'

With that I got into the car and drove off, wondering if I would ever see the place again. I cursed the fact that Brian Bonner had not attended the management seminar that might have given him a chance to grasp what it was all about.

How much of British management is like what I found at Videoprint? I think the answer may be: far too much. Throughout the eighties managements were given 'freedom to manage' and the chance to demonstrate that they knew what they were doing. Sadly, things got worse if anything.

In the seventies, working conditions like those at Videoprint would have been virtually impossible. No trade union would have agreed to such long shifts and to the switching back and forth between day shift and night shift, week in and week out. Now that trade union power is much diminished, the Videoprint management was free to dictate that those hours would be worked – helped by higher levels of local unemployment.

The management seemed to have very little appreciation of what the long shifts meant to the workers. One of the most revealing remarks I overheard came from one of the managers, who told a team member that he himself had worked the shift system at first but was glad that was behind him: it was 'just too knackering'. It was all right for the operatives, he said, because they were used to it! The fact that there was a high turnover of labour at Videoprint seemed to have given the management no sense of the true feelings of the people who worked there.

Too many British companies have a blind spot when it comes to the benefits that businesses derive from treating people as people and not as some mechanical part of the process. Machines can't think, can't work out better ways of doing things, and often create waste rather than eliminate it. Everywhere I went at Videoprint I could see examples of the Japanese concept of Muda – waste of materials, of time, of people's talents. A concentrated programme of empowering the workers, giving them responsibility for improvement and increasing their job satisfaction, would have paid such high dividends that the shift system could have been replaced by something more civilized. And people less tired and more enthusiastic would deliver better quality and better value for money. Why do so few managers in Britain recognize this simple truth?

After the bruising encounter with Brian Bonner, the plan to return to Videoprint with the television cameras some months later became a delicate matter of negotiation between the television production team and the factory management. Videoprint was clearly worried about the impact of the TV programme on their image and they pressed to be shown the film in advance – something that the television team was not prepared to concede. Eventually the idea of a TV return to the factory had to be put aside.

My own view was that there could be no progress without a major change in the management's attitude. However, when the research team returned five months later to assess the situation they were surprised to find that the company was now committed to introducing many of the ideas we had discussed. The company continued to be profitable and indeed had expanded considerably. A consultant had been brought in to train the entire factory in the techniques of continuous improvement, based on teamwork. On paper it all looked very impressive. Managers were to be assessed on their skills at people management and trained to be more supportive. 'Improvement teams' were to be formed and given Japanese-style problem-solving techniques. It was all going to cost the company a lot of money. However, not a lot had been done and a quick survey of the workforce found very little evidence that there had been, as yet, any fundamental change in management attitudes.

It would be nice to think that the showdown at Videoprint had at least started a process that would lead on to better things. Lee Paterson genuinely seemed to be in favour of change. Crucially, it would depend on the determined backing of top management to push the change through.

I sincerely hope they will succeed.

CHAPTER THREE

A NEW DAWN IN RAWTENSTALL

whatever future people can conceive and believe, they can achieve

Our second company was two hundred miles away in Lancashire, and was a total contrast to Videoprint. Whereas Videoprint could be regarded as an advanced technology company, Lambert Howarth was in one of Britain's oldest manufacturing industrial sectors. It also had a completely different management style at the top.

Lambert Howarth's Greenbridge footwear factory is located in Rawtenstall, one of the old mill towns that had sprung up about two hundred years ago to take advantage of the plentiful supply of water-power. Those early temples to mass production, the cotton mills, produced cotton thread in bulk for a few large customers in the weaving mills north of Manchester. It was an undemanding market, where price was the most important factor. To serve it, the mill-owners created the model of production that gave Britain a world lead in the nineteenth century but which proved woefully inadequate for the changing conditions of the twentieth.

The workers (or 'hands') were employed to do
simple, repetitive tasks that didn't require them
(or allow them) to use their brains. The man in
charge (the 'charge-hand') was supposed to do all
the thinking that was necessary, keeping the workforce
under control through strong discipline and the threat of sacking.

Understandably, the workers didn't care much for the job or for the
charge-hand and probably felt no more well-disposed to the mill-owner.
The hierarchical organization of the factory was reflected in the physical
layout and social life of the valley, with the mill-owner living in the large
house on the hill, the charge-hands in more modest but comfortable
houses lower down the slopes, and the workers huddled together in
crowded terraces stretching along the valley.

These thoughts had passed through my head as I stood on the terrace
of my hotel in Rawtenstall, possibly once a mill-owner's mansion, and
looked out over the town before paying my first visit to the former cotton
mill that now housed Lambert Howarth's shoe factory. There I was due to
meet the managing director to discuss whether my 'heroes' approach
could turn the place around.

Barry Forester, newly appointed MD at forty, greeted me warmly at
Reception and conducted me on a guided tour of the old mill. As we
went, he explained how he had come to be there and what he hoped to
achieve. Until a few weeks earlier he had been managing director of Dawes
Cycles in Birmingham. At Dawes, a pale shadow of its former self when
he took over in 1986, he had achieved something of a turnaround, using
some Japanese ideas.

As I have hinted at before, the genius of the Japanese had been to
realize that in the modern industrial economy it was the companies which
best served the increasingly sophisticated customer's real or perceived
needs which would come out on top. They saw it in terms of quality, cost
and delivery. The company which produced the highest quality goods or
services – in terms of design, reliability and variety of choice – and did this

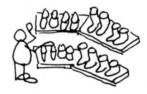

at the lowest cost and with the fastest delivery, was bound to take business from the opposition. The customer would be not just satisfied but delighted with the product or service. And if you could deliver customer delight, then the customer would not only come back for more but also pass on the good news to others.

At Dawes Barry Forester had made a big impact, but it had taken him a long time to steer the company culture away from 'command and control management' and 'them and us' divisions, and towards a new model based on consultation and consensus, with everyone working as a team. He was particularly proud of having phased out a piecework system that made it difficult to introduce new working practices and new models.

At the Rawtenstall shoe factory he didn't think he had as much time to improve the situation. The company supplied a range of shoes and slippers to a few big customers – big names like Marks and Spencer, K Shoes and Clarks. But its markets were under threat as never before. Factories in China were producing similar footwear, which was being imported into Europe at discounted prices. There was stiff competition, too, from within Europe. Together these rivals put Lambert Howarth under great pressure both to cut costs and to improve quality.

In 1971 the company had employed two thousand people in the Rossendale Valley; that number was now down to just over three hundred. The story is only too familiar in Britain. In the last year alone one of the Rossendale factories had been closed and the operation concentrated at the Greenbridge factory. 'It has had an effect on morale,' Barry told me, 'and I think made it more of a challenge to turn the operation around. But I believe we can do it. I have not come here to see the business fold, but to get it back on its feet and create new jobs.' This, of course, was music to my ears.

Although he had been there only a matter of weeks, Barry Forester had already set his sights on moving upmarket, producing better-quality products and – most fundamental of all – exploiting the firm's advantage in being close to its main customers. 'Let me put it this way,' he said, 'if you import from China you have to place orders in large batches considerably in advance of actually selling them on. If the market changes, if styles change, you can have your fingers burnt. What we want to do is to be able to react quickly to the market needs of our customers. We want to be able to develop new products with better design input and provide a higher level of service.'

To achieve this would mean scrapping the very traditional approach to manufacturing that I could see all around me. It was like taking a trip into the past. The workbenches were laid out in neat rows, and shoes and slippers – in various stages of manufacture – progressed along the rows in batches of dozens at a time. In addition, the workforce operated on a piecework system whereby wages are directly related to the quantity produced. While I don't consider money the best motivation – that comes from feeling valued as a human being – bad pay systems certainly wreck attempts to make factories better places to work and therefore more efficient. If we were going to create a flexible workspace here – designed to allow small batch production and to facilitate the nimbleness required to meet the needs of more discriminating customers – the piecework system would have to go.

In place of the old-style production flow, which lacked the ability to switch easily from one mode of production to another as orders came in, what was needed here was Japanese-style cellular manufacturing. Not, however, according to the textbooks on the Japanese system – often written by Western 'experts' who are book-wise but lack intuitive understanding – but according to the needs of the workforce who would have to run it. The workers could be trusted to design it themselves, make it work and continually improve it – though only if they were involved from the start.

Cellular manufacturing is one of those ideas that have been brought over from Japan and applied with mixed success in Britain. This is because the principles have been poorly understood and implemented from the top down, depriving the operators of any initiative and any ownership of the process. Only recently I read of a factory where the workers came back from the weekend to find that the management had rebuilt the factory on cellular manufacturing principles. How do we think the workers looked on it? And guess how many simple mistakes in the design the managers would have made?

before   after

It is easy to design a cell in theory – like the one illustrated. But only the real experts who do the job day in, day out can understand the finer touches. The Rawtenstall factory offered a good opportunity to introduce the idea to a workforce which had always worked the traditional way, and to show them what a difference it would bring about. It would make their job easier and much more fun. As a result products would be produced faster and be of better quality.

I left Rawtenstall fairly confident that we could find the heroes and start the process of bouncing back. In a way the whole economy of the area, and the hopes of future job opportunities for the people there, depended upon it.

But later at the Manchester conference where all the companies participating in the programmes were represented, I encountered the Greenbridge factory's production director, Gary Smith, and the factory manager, Brian Hodson. Although they were nice enough people, their reaction to some of the new management ideas that we discussed was a little worrying. Like Brian Bonner at Videoprint, they were inclined to think that supervisors had the best ideas; they felt that the workers were only there to do what management required of them, and could contribute little more. But, unlike at Videoprint, here in Barry Forester we had an MD who was determined to make things happen, and who realized that the workforce had a key role to play.

DAY ONE

The weather was grey and misty as I unloaded the workshop kit and carried it into the 'training centre' laid aside for the two-day exercise in industrial improvement at Lambert's. It was seven o'clock in the morning, and people were already passing by on their way to work.

The Rossendale Valley in Lancashire had many of the characteristics of Britain's older industrial areas. The stone-built terraces – built to withstand cold, damp, windy winters – housed a traditional working-class community. The very geography of the place helped to give people a sense of solidarity and fostered a supportive culture. In that sense it was very like Armley in Leeds, where I had grown up. Outsiders – especially Yorkshire folk (I considered myself a missionary on this particular workshop)– can be treated with suspicion and find it difficult to gain acceptance. Barry Forester, I imagined, must be facing this handicap too. But if he showed he had the interests of Lambert's and the local people at heart, then in my experience he would find them an enormous asset – hard-working, loyal, and capable of taking on and beating any workers in the world. Those who despair about Britain's future as an industrial nation should remember that it was workers like the people of Rawtenstall who made Britain the 'Workshop of the World' – the industrial giant of the nineteenth century.

There is no reason to believe that their present-day descendants cannot deliver in the same way, if only we give them a chance.

Easier said than done, you might think. We take the attitude: let's not proceed until we have laid the groundwork....We need to consult psychologists and personnel specialists to work out new forms of assessment, better pay systems, structured training courses, long-term development plans. This sort of thing can take years. But one major objection to this Western intellectual and analytical approach is that by the time we've done it the business may have gone to the wall (remember the road roller behind you), or at the very least been 'down-sized' to keep it competitive.

Yet if we tap into the wisdom of Zen we will realize that it is the act of doing that leads on to understanding, and that understanding leads on to doing things better, which leads on to greater understanding. While we have been analyzing ourselves into oblivion, the Japanese have just been getting on with the job.

didn't mother say, practice makes perfect?

And while I am on the subject I think every manager in Britain should be made to read that very revealing book, *The Tao of Pooh*. It was the author's genius to see that Pooh came off best because he went with the flow; 'wise' Owl, unfortunately, is the model for most of our industrial leaders.

By eight o'clock the workshop teams had settled down round their tables. Barry Forester, accompanied by Brian Hodson and Gary Smith, put in an appearance to introduce me. Over the two days, he told the assembled workers, people on the workshop were to be set free to come up with their own ideas of how to improve the factory. At four o'clock the next day the management team would be coming back to be 'gobsmacked' by the results. Sid, he said, had assured him of that. 'So I am handing you over to Sid for two days, and good luck!'

As the door closed behind the three managers I had my first chance to get to know the twenty-odd workers, all from an area in the factory rather quaintly referred to as the 'closing room'. This did not mean that it was next on the list for the chop – it was in fact the department that sewed together the individual parts of felt slippers. The workers were almost 100 per cent female, completely unsentimental about the prospect of going through a course for two days, and about as enthusiastic as turkeys lining up for Christmas.

As I passed round the sticky labels for people to write their names, or nicknames, on them (names that you can own up to in public, I joked), I felt the pressure of their sceptical gaze. Who was I? Some sort of management stooge? Some con artist who would wheedle them into changing the way they did things, only to see jobs lost and wages cut? (Oh dear, what damage all those well-meaning consultants have done to workplace attitudes.) Already I felt myself sweating under the heat of the television lights.

Workshops often begin with a wall of hostility being thrown up. The Bullshit Repellent can raise a laugh and get across the message that I am no normal 'consultant', but I usually have a two-hour slog before I get accepted. People who have been abused and deceived over the years and never been shown trust or respect of any sort have every right to put up a solid front of non-cooperation. The irony is that most managers don't appreciate that they abuse, deceive and distrust people: they see taking a hard line on working practices, lateness and suspected pilfering on the factory floor as an integral part of their job. But none of these things is a problem if we build workplace teams and hand them responsibility for keeping people in line. In the case of Lambert's the flow of bile coming from the workshop members was about as bitter and poisonous as I have ever come across.

Leading the sceptics was Hannah Garrard, a woman with a powerful personality and a natural leader. To Hannah, the outcome of the workshop would be just the same as on previous exercises of this type: 'Management will knock our wages back, just like they did before.' To her, the piecework system was not to be surrendered lightly. She was a good worker and earned more than the average wage of £160 a week. Although her husband Fred had a job in a shoe factory across the street she had no wish to see her income fall as a result of some jumped-up consultant's idea.

Although it was never stated during the workshop, there was also an obvious fear that changes in working practices might lead to a cut in the labour force. And, heaven knows, there had been enough redundancies lately (250 jobs had gone when the two factories had been rationalized into one just three months previously).

Throughout the morning I battled away, teaching them the basics of world-class manufacture, telling them of the new world where they would be treated as 'experts' in what they did and would play a vital role in beating off the opposition and putting Lambert's on the map. I gave them assurances that management had agreed to my pre-condition that there would be no redundancies as a result of the changes, and told them I had it in writing.

From time to time I seemed to be on the edge of a breakthrough. I could not undo the past, but we could build a new future based on mutual respect, a restoring pride in the workplace, and on the teams sorting out the problems that they all knew existed but had never been able to do anything about. Then, just when the teams seemed on the point of buying into the vision, the whole question of money would resurface.

By midday I was feeling the strain. I snapped at them that they had the choice: they could leave the workshop if they wanted but, if they stayed on, they would have to agree to give it a try. Hannah reacted very badly to the idea, and there were mutterings in support. The lunch break came none too soon.

Of course, all these proceedings were being filmed – and you can imagine my concerns. The magic had always worked for me on my own, but now a TV camera and lights were making it clear that this was a special occasion. Were the teams acting up for the benefit of the camera? Was there an inner tension showing through my outwardly relaxed and joking self? And would it stop the flow of Tao and Zen?

Over a sandwich I decided that, like it or not, it was up to management to make that extra gesture. Time was running out, and without a new initiative on their part the magic that I wanted to release from within these people would remain stubbornly locked away. So when we reassembled in the training room I asked one of the group to go to the MD's office and ask him to come across. Within five minutes Barry Forester was back in front of the workshop teams. He seemed genuinely surprised, and quipped: 'I thought I'd given you to Sid for two days!'

I explained the problem: the groups needed some guarantees about the effect on pay. To his credit, Barry did not equivocate. He said that if the new cells were built there would be no loss of earnings. He would take the average earnings of each person under the piecework system, and that would become their new pay rate: as for redundancies, they were not on the agenda.

Barry Forester was new to these women and came from a totally different cultural background. He spoke English with what we in the North would regard as a cultivated southern accent. Before that morning they had never met him, so it was perhaps understandable that they felt some reluctance to take everything he said as the gospel truth. However, the very fact that he had been prepared to make the trip over to the training centre in person marked him out as a new style of MD – more approachable, apparently concerned enough about the feelings of the staff to leave off what he was doing and put in an appearance.

After he had gone I felt we could finally get started on the job I had come to do: to give them a grasp of the principles of designing and building cells, so that they would have the confidence to go out and do just that the following morning. 'I won't be designing the cells or supervising what you'll do,' I told them. 'We won't be following any blueprint designed by some fancy consultant. You will have the job to do, and by doing it you will surprise even yourselves at the pool of expert knowledge you possess and which no one has ever tapped before.'

By five o'clock we had laid the groundwork. Each team had its supply of charts and stopwatches and was ready to get out there and start designing the cells. But although I had broken the ice and got most of the women on my side there was still something missing. They laughed at my jokes (at least some of them did) and forgave me, I hope, my odd naughty word, but under the surface I detected that the sceptics were still to be convinced. Could I do more? I couldn't see that I could. I would just have to keep my fingers crossed and hope that everything would go like clockwork in the morning.

That evening I discussed the day's events with the programme production team who had discovered Lambert Howarth's and Barry Forester and decided that they should feature in the series. I was only just beginning to realize that the production team's agenda and mine were not the same. They thought the drama of that day's events would make excellent television, all the more effective because it would make a nice contrast with my eventual triumph: they were sure I would win through in the end. My worry was that the whole enterprise had been put at risk by the presence of the cameras. And, while I had told them to find me an average bunch of workers who could be won over to the new way of thinking, I suspected that they had selected the most difficult characters in the factory if only to make better TV.

The producers felt my fears were groundless. People in Rawtenstall were naturally sceptical, they argued, and were concerned that change would be to their disadvantage. They had got to know the people in the factory much better than I had, and even the 'cynical' Hannah (my view: I felt she had given me a particularly hard time) was a sweetie at heart. It was just that I had never met her outside the work situation.

Of course, from the start the idea had been that I should not meet any of the companies or the people involved before the filming took place. Since I had never met them and had no part in selecting who should be involved in the workshop, it ought to prove my strongly held belief that there is magic in everyone if only we know how to bring it out. But that evening I couldn't help wondering if the whole concept of uncovering this magic under the stern eye of the television camera was seriously flawed. Before going to bed I made my usual phone call to Jean. Even so, I didn't sleep well that night.

DAY TWO

As the women came bustling into the training centre the next morning Barry Forester was already on site, armed with a piece of paper. This time he had his managers with him – possibly a shrewd move, as both sides would hear what he had to say. He set about quelling the workers' residual fears in a forthright manner.

'The first thing to say is there's not much point in doing this if all we're going to do is shit on you. As Sid will have told you, this is about working together and working as a team.' He waved a sheet of paper in the air. 'This piece of paper says that when we put people in cells they'll go on average earnings. If you like, it freezes the current situation.' Everybody, he assured them, would get this guarantee.

I watched the faces as Barry's words registered. In all the years of the factory's existence there had probably never been an occasion when the managing director had come down among the workers to speak to them as a group, not once but three times in the course of twenty-four hours. Hannah and the rest of what I considered to be the awkward squad seemed genuinely impressed.

It was now up to them. As always, I stayed behind in the conference room when the groups of workers set out on their voyage of exploration through the company, looking for ways in which it was wasting materials, money and human talent.

Twenty women had spent eight hours with me on Day One. Most of that time had been expended in complaining about the past and worrying about the future. All in all I had managed about two hours of practical exercises on the principles of cell manufacturing. Despite that, they were now setting about the task with growing confidence and enthusiasm. The explanation for this success comes from an ancient Chinese proverb: Tell me and I'll forget; show me and I may remember; involve me and I'll understand. These heroes were now fully involved.

tell me and I'll forget; show me and I may remember; involve me and I'll understand

They began by 'walking the job' – timing operations, separating value-adding operations from the rest. That alone was an eye-opener. It involved penetrating parts of the factory they had never worked in as well as more familiar haunts. Everywhere they found Muda in all its forms.

There were the familiar wastes: of materials, in the form of defects; of manpower, as people hung about doing nothing, waiting for materials; and of time, as machines broke down or lay idle. But there were also unfamiliar and often unrecognized aspects of waste – of unnecessary movement, of stock being tied up, of over-production (yes, that is a form of waste!), of the production process itself, and most of all the waste of people's talents. Added together, all this can treble or quadruple production costs: using the talents of the workforce to eliminate waste saves far more money and makes lots more sense than sacking them in a cost-cutting operation. But too few of Britain's business leaders seem to recognize this fundamental truth.

During the course of the morning I met Hannah. She seemed very excited as she got to grips with the real production problems that had bedevilled the factory for years. 'We don't see this side of it,' she told us as the team surveyed the other departments. 'The work just sat there, didn't it?' She pointed to a bin full of half finished shoes. 'That's where half the money's going. And that's why we can't have rises.'

Once the waste survey was completed, the teams applied their newly acquired techniques of waste elimination with mounting enthusiasm. Just as I had learnt from Chihiro Nakao in Japan that to do was to solve, the women grasped the need to rearrange the machines to smooth production flows, cut down lead times and make the job a lot easier to do. It never ceases to amaze me that people with precious little to show for their formal education can tackle jobs that were once the domain of qualified production engineers – and do it better, simply because they have an intuitive understanding of the process. The only thing the Lambert Howarth's people lacked that afternoon was the physical strength.

At their suggestion I spoke to Barry, Gary and Brian, the all-male top management team, and asked them to help move the machines. It not only gave them some useful physical exercise, it did more for industrial relations in that factory in half an hour than a month of meetings between management and unions could have achieved. As the managers arrived to help and were supervised by our 'experts', you could almost feel the suspicion and resentment of years starting to melt away.

By 3.30 p.m. the new machine layout was in place and the first test was all set to run. The women found it had taken three weeks to make a slipper under the old method: using the new cell it took exactly 45 seconds! The distance travelled fell from 250 yards to just 15, and work in progress fell from 5000 pairs of slippers to just 12.

Barry Forester summed it all up: 'Wandering round this shop before, I wouldn't have said it looked like things were going slowly. It looked a quick shop. This is absolutely staggering.' He could have added, 'Without expending any more than our people's time and our muscle-power to help out.' One of the basic principles behind the workshops, as I explained earlier, is that none of the improvements must cost money. And if it costs nothing to implement, company accountants – or, as I prefer to refer to them, 'bean counters' – don't get to veto or postpone the change.

There was applause all round. I looked over and caught a glimpse of Hannah. She had been transformed in my mind from 'Hannah the Horrible' to 'Hannah the Hero'. There was a flush of triumph on the faces of Hannah and all the team members. It is very humbling to witness the effect on people when their talents are unleashed. For me, and for them, it seems an almost spiritual experience. Happiness is infectious, laughter opens the gates of the mind to learning, and it is all reinforced by the fact that it is a group experience. Why have we in Britain taken so long to learn these simple principles of Zen?

or is it Zen? didn't mother say laughter is the best medicine?

It was 4.30p.m. on Day Two and I was packing the gear into the back of the Peugeot. Time to consider the lessons of the two days. The nightmare start seemed a long way off. My fears that the TV cameras would stop the magic happening, and the depths of cynicism I had encountered, had all turned out to be unimportant. Somehow, once the process gets going, nothing seems to be able to stop it. The magic is always the same.

However, the production team and I would be coming back three months later to see if the process begun so dramatically had been kept going. That was a daunting prospect. Normally I prepare management teams for the challenge, since many managers find the process of real worker empowerment very unsettling and very threatening. It must be irksome to see changes implemented in a day that you had not been able to achieve in years of trying. Many managers convey their disbelief through body language rather than words. They stand arms folded and grim-faced as the worker teams unfold their achievements. It conveys the belief: it's all done with mirrors, and it certainly won't last.

In many companies the changes don't last because it is all too easy for managers to stop things happening, to sap the enthusiasm of the teams through ill-considered language or the aggressive reassertion of authority. So what would happen after my car was loaded up, the television crew was speeding down the motorway, and Hannah and her heroes had to face the managers on their own?

One reassurance was the commitment of Barry Forester, a man who had genuinely seen the light. He had regarded the television programme as a way of effecting rapid cultural change at Lambert Howarth's. He was just as committed as I was to the survival and revival of British manufacturing. But he had to operate in a fierce, cut-throat market where only the fittest were going to survive. I had to put my trust in him and hope that, when we came back, the revolution we had started would still be rolling on.

The spring snow had long vanished as I drove across the Pennines again into the Rossendale Valley. The sun shone brightly and added an optimistic dimension. But would the changes at Rawtenstall have taken root and flourished?

The research team had kept in touch with the factory and with some of the heroes. They believed that progress was being maintained, and there had been some further changes, but they were suspiciously vague on the details. Only seeing for myself would enable me to judge whether this was clever PR by the company (we are masters of putting the most optimistic sheen on outcomes) or real and lasting change.

In particular I was seriously concerned that the management team had not been trained in the new approach and that we had not been able to brief the whole workforce about what the changes meant. Factories and offices are wonderful rumour machines: Chinese whispers sweep through the corridors and across the shop-floor; sinister motives are ascribed when none exist. No group of workers likes to take the role of management lackey, and that in itself can stop the changes in their tracks.

In the event I was bowled over by what we found. Hannah Garrard now had an almost benign attitude towards me. When I remarked on her change of view, she countered that I had not always come over as totally sympathetic to their cause. Maybe that was true. Workers who open themselves to productivity improvement are often betrayed by managements too short-sighted to see the harm they do with their resort to immediate job-shedding. Had I been a worker at Lambert's would I have taken the chance?

The factor that had swung Hannah and the other workers behind the project had not been me, nor Barry Forester's piece of paper (worthy though it was), but the experience of actually going out and doing it for themselves. They had experienced the liberating feeling of getting the bosses off their backs and taking decisions for themselves.

Since my visit, the groups had completed three more cells and were working on others. The new cell layout was even better than those we had designed on the workshop. This is a common experience. While the first cell had been a dramatic improvement on the previous system, it was no more than a first attempt. Once workers know how to uncover the causes of inefficiency, faulty production and slow delivery, they can go on improving the way they do things again and again.

In Japan it is known as Kaizen: this can be roughly translated as 'improving goodness', but the translation does not catch the philosophy behind the approach. In the West, we now call it 'continuous improvement'. It is the key to the progression of Toyota motor cars from pale copies of American models in the sixties to the superb vehicles they are today. The idea of continually improving by small steps rather than by the great technological leaps that appeal to our macho culture lies at the heart of the difference between Japanese achievement and relative failure of Western business.

The new cells at Lambert's, designed by the operator teams, conformed to the four principles of the Sid Joynson approach to Kaizen: To make everyone's job easier, faster, safer, and have fun. And although the factory had only just begun its journey there was no disguising the air of progress, of greater happiness, of pride in achievement.

On the management side Barry Forester, too, looked pretty pleased with himself. He reported that productivity was up 25 per cent in one department, that defects in its product had fallen from 7 per cent to zero, and that generally the improved quality of the production and the ability to switch quickly from one line of production to another was already attracting new customers. My concerns about Brian Hodson and Gary Smith proved to be mistaken. Since the day that the two managers had come on to the factory floor to move the machinery, a new relationship had been forged with the worker teams. Hannah confessed that she now thoght Gary and Brian 'quite decent blokes'!

Hannah's home life, too, had improved now that she was no longer treated as an 'unperson' at work. This was important, because it further confirms my belief that the sort of society we have outside the work situation is shaped by what happens in our working lives. People who are unhappy at work tend to take it out on others once they have passed out of the workgates.

Although this is important, we shouldn't forget the strong business message emerging from the Lambert Howarth experience that forms a fitting close to this chapter. Although the future of the factory had not yet been secured, the company had already found that shorter lead times, smaller production batches and better quality made sense when it came to delivering customer delight. If customers wanted a new style of slipper, perhaps in a new colour or in particular sizes, then they could get it. There was no way in which the Chinese slipper industry could match this level of service.

It sums up what people power in a business environment is all about.

CHAPTER FOUR

TAKING ON THE CHUNNEL

the only thing
we have to fear is
fear itself

As I drove along the M20 above Folkestone the signs announcing the Channel Tunnel were everywhere. Even so, the sheer size of the terminal came as a surprise. It lay there nestling in a hollow at the top of the cliffs, a massive vehicle reception area served by ramps and flyovers waiting to receive its first paying customers. It was June 1994 and the Tunnel was already over a year behind schedule. But within a few months the ramps would be opened, the massive shuttle trains would be waiting to receive the traffic, and Britain's status as an island would be gone for good.

The railway lines suddenly vanished into the gaping tunnel mouth and I found myself on the descent into Dover – home to the shortest Channel crossings and under most immediate threat. Dover is Britain's busiest ferry port and thousands of jobs depend on the ferry business.

When major tunnels and bridges have opened in the past, ferry services have been among the first casualties – think of the Humber, the Severn and the Forth. In 1987, when the Tunnel project was given the go-ahead, many people in Dover saw it as a delayed death sentence. One of the most famous ferry crossings in the world would be slowly throttled as passengers and freight switched to the convenience and speed of the Tunnel. Dover would be the biggest loser.

My workshop in Rawtenstall had shown that we can both save jobs and create new ones in manufacturing industry by harnessing the power of the workforce to the cause. Now I was determined to prove that the message was just as powerful for service industries. While technology and methodology can improve business, it is what I call peoplology that is so often the critical factor for success.

Since 1987 the ferry companies had been planning their strategy to beat off the challenge of the Tunnel. They would do it by changing the rules of the game. Sun T'su, that brilliant military strategist and tactician, wrote in 400 BC that a good general faced with a powerful enemy never fights on the enemy's chosen ground. The good general chooses the terrain that gives his people the best chance of victory. 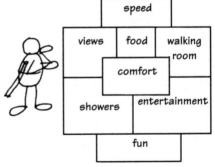 For ferry companies that meant competing not in terms of speed, where the Tunnel holds the high ground, but on a battlefield of their own choice – one where speed was a positive disadvantage. The Tunnel had chosen to offer customers a quick thirty-minute crossing in box-like wagons – an experience which had about as much charm as using a pedestrian underpass. The Channel ferries, on the other hand, could build on the traditions of the cruise liner and turn themselves into floating pleasure palaces complete with games rooms, shopping malls, fast food parlours, bars and restaurants – on the principle that the journey might be an hour or so longer but so much fun that it would be well worth the extra time.

The strategy would initially involve the existing fleet and additional vessels being introduced in the coming years. It depended too on developing the organization, offering quick check-in procedures well laid out facilities and so on. That's the methodology bit. But none of this grand scheme would work without involving the talents of the people running the terminals or working on the ferries, and without making sure they were not alienated by their working conditions or by the way they were managed. So peoplology holds the key.

These were my thoughts as I drew up at Dover's Eastern Docks and looked at the chosen object of my next workshop: the massive form of *Stena Invicta*, 20,000 tonnes, with the capacity to carry nearly 2000 passengers, 400 cars and 150 lorries or coaches. Over its four shifts it provided jobs for about 1600 people.

I had discussed the project with Ewan Park, Human Resources Director of Stena Sealink, the UK arm of the Scandinavian-owned Stena line, 'the world's largest ferry operator'. Ewan had impressed me as a man who saw the value of TLC – Tender Loving Care – in his approach to the workforce. 'We want our customers to find our ferries friendly, fun places. We're not going to achieve this unless we have a happy and committed staff, with jobs as secure as we can make them,' he told me. He also admitted that the company had a problem.

Stena Sealink was a comparatively new organization. Sealink had begun as a ferry service operated jointly by British Rail and the French and Belgian nationalized railway companies. In the early days of the post-war travel boom cross-Channel ferries had been seen as unglamorous workhorses. The important thing was to get from A to B, not the manner of getting there. Then in 1983 the British end of Sealink was privatized and sold to the British Company Sea Containers, run by a flamboyant Canadian businessman, James Sherwood. The going was tough as rivals like P & O emerged. P & O took over Townsend Thoresen, and invested in new, larger ferries.

Despite the growing threat of the Tunnel, the Swedish company, appeared on the scene in 1990 as a predator, eyeing up not just the Channel ferries but the extensive Sealink network elsewhere (it included Irish Sea ferries and the Harwich–Hook of Holland crossing). Sea Containers did not give up without a fight, a fact that must have pushed up the price that Stena had to pay. All this when the recession was biting hard and interest rates soaring. At the end of its first financial year Stena Sealink was faced with losses of £30 million.

The scars of 1991–2 linger on at Dover. The company had to take drastic action. Under a new managing director, Gareth Cooper, 'Operation Benchmark' was launched and there was a drastic slimming down exercise; 35 per cent of the staff were made redundant. It was as though the Channel Tunnel had come two years earlier than expected.

There is no doubt that this history was going to make my job that much harder. Here was a company whose words had spoken of a desire for job security, but whose deeds apparently told a different story. Ewan Park recognized the problem: 'It was a case of having to lose 35 per cent of the jobs to save the other 65 per cent. If we had not had 'Operation Benchmark', there would have been no jobs at all.'

The immediate hurdle I had to surmount would be the cynicism which the crews were bound to express. But I felt sure that could be achieved. I had dealt with worse situations in the past. I had often been called in following blood-lettings, possibly because while forced by the balance sheet to cut costs and to axe jobs, many companies also appreciate that the key to long-term success is to get the best out of the people who remain.

Finding the heroes here and setting them free was not going to be the easiest of assignments. But of course we would find them, and the managers would be astounded as usual. With that thought I went to bed, ready to start the workshop at eight the next morning, and taking with me some back numbers of the staff magazine *Online*. Glossy and well-produced, it gave me a flavour of the new vision the company wanted to create. The good news was that the company was now in the black and that passenger figures on the Dover–Calais route were up by over 10 per cent in 1993;

freight traffic, too, had continued to grow. Almost to emphasize how shrewd the company had been in buying into the UK ferry market, Stena Sealink had carried 13 per cent more passengers, while the Swedish ferries had suffered a drop of 18 per cent in the same year. But what really interested me was the centrepiece article on the Channel ferry strategy.

Stena now had two large, flagship ferries operating on the Dover–Calais route – the *Fantasia* and the *Invicta*. To meet the challenge of the Tunnel, both were being developed as new concept ferries. On the way out were the traditional naval clothes, to be replaced by informal American-style company uniforms. I could detect more than a hint of Disneyland about the whole approach.

The *Fantasia* was being used as a test bed for what the marketing department called the Globetrotter Food and Beverage Concept. It combined fast food – a bewildering range including a McDonald's restaurant, an Easy Diner and a Globetrotter Café – with trendy bars and a 'fun' approach. This involved a novel concept of how the staff should behave. The magazine solemnly told me that the staff 'should consider themselves to be on stage when they are working and their customers are the audience'. It went on: 'We want to create a permanent party atmosphere on board and to move away from a "speak when you're spoken to" attitude.' I had a mental image of the traditionally sombre deck-hand wearing a party hat and rushing up to welcome the startled passengers on board.

Seriously, though, the company was making a lot of the right kind of noises about tapping into the talents of the staff. 'The thing about Globetrotter is that there are no tablets of stone. It is the crew themselves who will create the new style... it was the crew's idea to have baseball caps... it is important that people feel involved.' Stena had put the crew of the *Fantasia* through a training programme to prepare them for 'a totally new way of working to encourage more interaction with the customer'.

This, of course, was very much a management-filtered view of the project. There was no way of telling how many staff reading the article might dismiss it as so much management twaddle. I did, however, notice one telling comment about staff reaction to the plan: '...there was a slight hesitancy in some quarters with a few "we've heard it all before" comments...'.

Just how much commitment was there inside the company to the grand new vision? Tomorrow I would begin to find out.

DAY ONE

It would have been nice to have conducted my entire workshop aboard the *Stena Invicta*. But with the ferry shuttling back and forward ten times a day, and limited room on board for conference-style meetings, it had been decided to spend the first day of the two-day bash ashore in the Moat House Hotel.

I had wanted a cross-section of ship and shore staff, all taken from the same shift. The twenty people taking part had been drawn from six areas: fourteen were from the ship's crew, while the remaining six were shore-based. When I first met them in the hotel's large conference room they looked an impressive bunch.

The crew members ranged from traditional sailors through to 'retail' staff who would look at home in any big fashion store. They had chosen not to wear company uniforms for the two-day session because they wanted to be themselves – a decision I applauded. Still, they were a far cry from my more regular heroes. In factory environments, at least to start with, my workshop members are often fairly reticent, curious to discover who I am and what I stand for, and not yet aware of their own huge potential. But the group before me now were ready from the start to express themselves in no uncertain terms.

I conjured up an image of Dover as the scene of former British triumphs. It was in the skies above here that the Luftwaffe was seen off in 1940. What had given the British the advantage in 1940? We were outnumbered, standing alone against the might of Hitler's Germany. Why did we think we could win? Because we held the moral high ground. In the 1990s there was still a war going on, and we were still under constant bombardment.

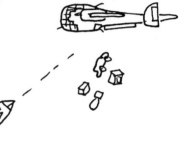

This time the enemy was dropping not bombs but cars, electrical goods, toys and many other products. This attack was destroying just as many factories as the bombs of the Luftwaffe had done – possibly even more. The casualties so far exceeded 2 million jobs killed. We needed to start fighting back, just as we had done in 1940.

For Stena Sealink there were two enemies that threatened their future. There was the Tunnel, which would eventually get its act together. That was a gigantic threat. But we should not forget that P & O were a threat too. We lived in a competitive world and we had to view them as a deadly enemy. Either we had to keep ahead of them, or they would get us too. The way to do that was continuously to get better, to delight customers more than the opposition did, and the only way to guarantee that was to tap into the intuitive skills of the real experts – the people who did the various jobs.

So far, so good. But, as so often, there was an air of latent cynicism that still had to come out into the open. It did so when I took one of the first questions.

'If we come up with better ways of doing things, how can we be sure we won't be putting ourselves out of a job?' I had already pulled out the Bullshit Repellent can and put it on the table in front of me.

'I'm glad you raised that point,' I said. 'Before coming here to speak to you I made it an absolute condition that there must be no question of anybody being made redundant as a result of any improvement you make.'

They didn't know me, or of my track record of walking out on companies I felt I couldn't trust. There was a round of cynical laughter. Gavin Williams, one of the ship's engineers, got up from his seat at the front and, in the nicest possible way, picked up the BSR and sprayed me with it.

If only managements could see what they do to people when they announce a round of redundancies. The reservoir of goodwill evaporates and the stream of ideas that ought to flow from it inevitably dries up. During my workshops I often draw a boat to represent the average British business – with the management at one end and the workers at the other, shooting their cannon at each other instead of at the enemy. I do so not

simply to point out the existence of 'them and us' culture, but because we have to do something about it. And by 'we' here I mean the managers. Treating staff as a mere 'cost' that can be disposed off in hard times is the first form of management behaviour that has to be changed. There's no sentimentality involved here – even though I believe that everyone deserves a decent job with a decent wage. No – my main reason for pushing for this kind of change is that productivity improves. That means that management benefits... and so does the company... and so does industry in general – in fact, everyone benefits.

In the case of Stena Sealink I knew we could overcome the negative effect of the earlier compulsory job losses, though it was going to take time. But I was scarcely prepared for what was to come next. Mentioning redundancies opened old wounds, but even more threatening to the natural functioning of this particular workshop was an ongoing source of deep resentment.

Stena had introduced a new method of working, drawn from their experience on the Swedish ferries. They had introduced twelve-hour shifts on a seven days on, seven days off basis, offering a superficially attractive deal of crews having every second week off. (In fact, with four weeks' annual holiday it meant twenty-eight weeks a year off!) But there was a considerable snag. Although each shift lasted at least twelve hours the crew members had to stay on board for the rest of the twenty-four-hour period. It was like working on an oil-rig far from home – but in a sense worse, since the ship actually called into the home port of Dover every few hours. Gavin Williams explained some of the discomforts that had to be endured. The crew had to sleep on board with tannoys blaring and engines vibrationing as the ship was manoeuvred in and out of port. 'It's hard to get uninterrupted sleep,' he said. 'What you find yourself doing is cat-napping. Maybe 90 per cent of the people who work here would rather be home every night.'

And it wasn't just home that they missed, as Shona Berry, who worked in the duty-free shop, pointed out. 'You don't get any fresh air, which plays havoc with your skin. You can't play any team games, because you can't turn out regularly every week. You can't do any night classes. The only thing that's good about it is that you save £30 a week on petrol!'

Michael Highnett, the ship's bosun, summed up the resentment felt about a shift pattern that had been imposed by management, albeit in the face of a company emergency: 'My wife absolutely hates it. She can't understand it. Nor can I.'

At a time when local unemployment is very high, many of the Sealink workers felt they were lucky to have a job of any kind. But the shift policy was very shaky ground on which to build the new 'customer-focused' company. And, of course, it was going to make my job over these two days all the harder. Still, it is remarkable how workforces can be pulled round to contribute to a company's strategy once they feel they are being treated not as paid slaves (I exaggerate for effect, but you can see the point) but as respected members of a team to which everybody belongs.

In reply to the tides of unhappiness over the shift system I told them that the best way forward was to try to push the past behind us, and paint a vision of what the new team-based company could be like. 'I would cry you a bucket of tears if it would help,' I sympathised, 'but we can't change the past. We can't guarantee the future. All we can tackle is the present and get that straight. When you present the results of your two days' work to the management tomorrow afternoon they'll be so amazed that they'd be idiots not to see that things have got to change.'

After lunch we really got down to doing the business. In the ship environment we weren't dealing with cellular manufacturing techniques, or change-over times on machines (although we could have analyzed the change-around time for the ferry if that had been a problem high on the agenda). We were dealing here with the issue of how to deliver not customer satisfaction but delight. And these heroes who had to deal with customers every day on a busy channel ferry held the secrets of how to deliver that delight.

The difference between my approach and the approach under trial on the *Fantasia* was that mine would not be seen as a top-down management initiative with 'experts' in customer care and marketing brought in to introduce new ideas and to try and 'involve' the staff in helping the managers develop and implement them. Consultancy on that basis is often poor value for money. It works for a while, with an outward warmth towards customers, but the staff really only go through the motions, since the ideas do not come from the real experts at the customer interface. Their hearts are not in it, and sooner or later the mask is bound to slip.

At the *Invicta* workshop I explained the basis of the Japanese Kaizen problem-analysis and problem-solving system. First you have to gather the facts and stick them up for all to see; then you come up with solutions, tapping into everybody's intuitive understanding. Once the possible solutions emerge they have to be tested and scrapped or amended in the light of that testing. It's as simple as that. It's not rocket science – just plain common sense.

Aboard the *Invicta* there were plenty of negative views about passengers – the 'customers' – that we had to dispose of first. The growth in the number of passengers carried is partly a reflection of the crazy situation created by what is supposed to be a single European market. The Dover–Calais crossing is ideal for those who want to make a quick day trip to enjoy French ambience and food. But a large number of these passengers don't go to see the sights or dine in a Michelin-starred restaurant. They get no further than the Calais hypermarkets, where bottles of cheap, rather weak beer (you can't trust the brand name because the brewers change the formula according to the country) are piled up in walls of cartons. The shoppers load up their hatchbacks and vans with as much as they can carry and take it back on the next ferry. Back home, much of it is sold 'off the back of a lorry' or at car boot sales. The practice has become so widespread that it is seriously undermining the pub trade in Britain. (Try counting the vans queuing up to get on the ferries at the weekends.)

Of course, nobody can blame the ferries for cashing in on the bonanza: the demand is there for crossing the Channel and they aim to satisfy it. But it does create problems for the staff as passengers come pouring back. Some are rude, bad-mannered and apt to throw up at the first sight of a wave – hardly the ideal customer whom the staff are expected to delight.

Shona Berry had had mixed experiences in the duty-free shop. 'The nice customers are the little old lady and man who have never been abroad before, and they've bought a disposable camera to take to Paris. When they come back and tell you what they've seen and done, it's quite exciting. The downside is that you get angry passengers who just want to rip your head off and everything is always your fault and you can only go so far in making them satisfied.'

Perhaps the beer rush will die down, although the fact that Sainsbury's have opened in Calais partly to tap the market is hardly an encouraging sign. But Stena managers have to realize that encouraging the beer rush traffic does little for the image of the company and even less for the nerves of the staff.

However, a negative attitude towards customers is usually related to how the staff themselves feel inside. When customers find the staff rude and unhelpful it is often because managers have been rude and unhelpful to the staff in the first place. To explain just how fast attitudes and culture can be changed, I told the Sealink people my T-junction story.

Attitude A – Day One:

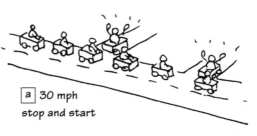

a 30 mph
stop and start

I drive up to a T-junction in the rush hour, and have to wait ten minutes to get out. When I do, it is not because someone lets me out – I just push in and make someone do an emergency stop. Now, knowing how difficult it was for me to get out, what am I going to do when I get to the next junction and find a driver in the same tricky situation? You're right – nothing. Why should I? Nobody helped me.

Attitude B – Day Two:

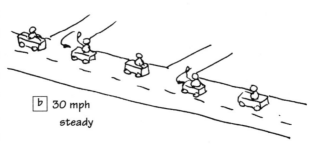

b 30 mph
steady

Same situation, but this time when I arrive at the junction, someone lets me out. I smile, they smile, and we all proceed. Now what do I do for the poor driver stuck at the next junction? You're right – I let him out. And, more importantly, guess how I feel about doing it?

We call this culture change method 'letting people out'. When we help each other the whole process flows smoothly, and even in a large business it could all be done in a day. The car held up at the first T-junction represents the staff, while the vehicle at the second one contains the customers. When the staff are let out by their managers they will automatically pass that gesture on to the customer. What we were trying to create here at Dover was a 'letting people out' approach. It pays dividends.

However, there was a further hiccup still to be dealt with before we could really settle down to show the managers what we could do. One of the information desk team, Sarah Kitchen, made a passionate point about the need for management to tackle the issue of temporary workers like herself. 'I give my everything to this company,' she said, and looked as though she meant it, 'but I get no holiday pay, no sick pay, and I can't get a mortgage. They say I'm temporary even though I've worked for the company for a year, and there's no sign of my being given a permanent job.'

In Britain more and more people are like Sarah – treated as temporary workers and given none of the employment rights enjoyed by permanent staff. When a company is up against it, as Sealink was, the option of taking on people on a temporary basis is attractive, especially if there are seasonal variations in demand. But temporary workers need to know exactly where they stand, otherwise they begin to feel exploited. And exploited people cannot be expected to perform as fully committed team members.

Despite all this, by three o'clock on Day One the magic inside these people was beginning to come out, almost despite themselves. Leading the way were the shore-based people, with the car-loading crew close behind. The loaders had already had some training in teamwork and saw that the Kaizen tools I was giving them could be put to good use. The rest of the crew were some distance behind, but not so far that they could never catch up.

It was DJ - the aimiable Scottish cafeteria worker, David Watts - who came to the rescue. During the workshops I always choose someone to be my 'assistant', the fall-guy who becomes the butt of my jokes. In DJ I had a willing collaborator, with just the right touch of humour. With his help I got through the planned programme, training every member of the workshop to be their own management consultant.

By the afternoon everybody seemed convinced that we could beat the Tunnel hands down. Who would want to spend half an hour in a dark tunnel, when they could be having a great time aboard a ferry? But we also had to remember that there were other enemies out there, such as P & O. Sun T'su wrote:

> Wise rulers and capable commanders win because they have advance information about the enemy. They know their enemy's strengths and weakness, as well as their own. The information cannot be obtained through supernatural force [or through reading the *Financial Times*], nor through conjecture [talking endlessly at board meetings about what the enemy is planning], nor through superstitious means [observing the share price of your rival]. Information can only be obtained from those who have a thorough knowledge of the enemy's conditions.

And who better to know than workers sent off on intelligence expeditions into enemy territory?

With a twinkle in my eye I announced the longer-term plan. We would be sending members of staff to travel on P & O ferries to take a note of every good idea they had and where they were doing better than us. We would bring this information back and copy their best ideas. Not only that – we would improve on them.

If we were doing everything as well as P & O and then made it better, where would that leave us? In the sixties British manufacturers complained that all the Japanese could do was to copy the West. They had no ideas of their own. But once they had done the copying they moved on. Who talks of Honda or Toyota or Sony copying now?

The practice of measuring yourself against the enemy is well known enough. It is called 'benchmarking'. Stena Sealink had already begun Operation Benchmark on the *Fantasia*, clearly with the intention of matching or beating the enemy. The trouble is that the people who do the benchmarking are not real experts. They are normally intelligent staff members, or management consultants, or maybe managers. Remember all those visits to Japan by businessmen in the seventies and eighties? What did that teach us? To misunderstand what Japan was all about. Now, if we had sent the real experts – people who had an intuitive understanding of what it was all about – to see how their counterparts did their jobs, how much better off we would be now!

By 5p.m. the plans were in place and we were all ready to roll next morning. This time we would be working not in a hotel conference room but on the *Invicta*.

DAY TWO

It was the first time I had been aboard the *Invicta* – I had made a deliberate point of not getting to know the ship before the workshop, in order to emphasize that the information and ideas came not from me but from the workshop teams. My first impressions were of a very large ship in which it would be easy to lose my bearings. It had all of ten decks and a bewildering number of stairways and lifts. There were four different types of restaurant offering food ranging from snacks to a full three-course meal, several bars, a video games area, a disco dance floor, shops and boutiques, and of course a gigantic duty-free emporium. It was mid-week mid-season, and the ship was spacious enough to seem quiet and uncrowded.

The plan was to form teams to go on fact-finding missions around the ferry. Some would 'walk the job': put themselves in the place of the passengers coming on board a strange ship, possibly tired, with children or elderly relatives, hungry or thirsty, out to shop, to disco, to relax, or maybe just to buy the duty-free. (Yes, because of recent changes in the regulations it was now possible to take a day trip to France and buy your duty-free allowances in both directions.) Other Sealink staff would conduct their own customer survey, speaking to car passengers, lorry drivers, coach drivers and so on, finding out what complaints they had and what changes they would like to see.

All this information was then brought back to our temporary conference room on board and put on charts. The survey found that most people were very satisfied with the service they were receiving on the *Invicta*, although there were complaints about the complexities of the duty-free regulations, about the food and about finding your way around.

'The point is,' I said, 'we need to do more than satisfy customers. We need to make sure we do all we can to delight them.'

What followed was the most interesting and productive part of the session, as more and more creative thoughts emerged on what they could do to delight customers so much that they would want to come back and to pass on recommendations to their friends. The transformation of moaning, dispirited people into glowing heroes out to dazzle the management was complete. I cannot explain it rationally. It has something to do with the spirit of Zen and the path of Tao. Once people get involved as teams in search of a common goal – a goal that seems both fair and good business sense – inner strengths are released, ideas flow, eyes gleam with passion and faces glow. After just four hours on the ferry we offloaded on to a bus that took us back to the Moat House Hotel.

At four o'clock the management team, led by Ewan Park, filed in. There were two company directors and about eight senior managers. If the teams felt nervous, it didn't show. One by one the spokespeople – DJ, Shona, Fiona Steward and Stuart Bryson – stood up and delivered confident summaries of the findings. There were forty recommendations in all.

The management team supported them all the way, and I am sure it was not just for the benefit of the cameras. The company had a record of good staff relations in Sweden, and had already begun to repair the damage caused by the emergency of 1991–2. The findings would be given very serious consideration by the board. This new spirit was what the company was trying to create. If it could be maintained, there was no doubt that the threat of the Channel Tunnel could be seen off.

Captain Cory, the senior officer (really the driver!) on the *Invicta*, spoke movingly about how impressed he had been by the presentations. He gave his wholehearted support to their efforts: 'Rest assured I shall implement things. We shall push forward from here.'

All I could remark on was the transformation. 'Where are those pissed-off people I had before me only a day ago? Gone, and I hope they never come back.' DJ summed it up. 'I'm trying hard not to be optimistic... we'll find out when you come back whether it's been accepted or not.'

Ten weeks later I came back to Dover to see if the momentum built up during the two-day workshop had been maintained. I passed through the airport-style reception area and was shuttled on to the ship by one of Stena's fleet of buses.

The most obvious difference was in the new signposts that had been put up at very little expense (remember, Kaizen workshops are not allowed to spend money to bring about improvements – it all has to be done by using the ingenuity and experience of the participants). The team members seemed happier in their jobs, filled with more gusto. The atmosphere and the relations within the company were certainly different.

I spoke to Ewan Park about the outcome. Of the forty suggestions, thirty-two had been adopted for action. He was particularly proud of the mock-up of the new *Welcome to the Invicta* leaflet, a guide to the ferry – an idea directly from the workshop. This, he assured me, was just the beginning.

In the cafeteria I came across DJ, my willing helper. He seemed in good spirits. He had got the new coffee machine he wanted, although that had in fact been agreed before the workshop session. But he did have two complaints. One was that not much had happened – not, at least, until the week before the TV team and I had been due to come back, and even then many of the decisions that had been taken in principle had 'Pending' set against them. DJ was also bewildered by the decision to cancel the orders for small trays. His team had suggested that customers would be much more comfortable, and probably buy more at the counter, if the trays were of a more generous size. But although the smaller ones had been dropped, there was no sign of new, larger ones!

I took the matter up with Nick Lyne, the hotel manager, and Mick Ambrose the training manager. The new larger trays were indeed on their way – it was just that nobody had thought to tell DJ. 'Gentlemen,' I counselled them, 'we have to think more about communication.'

I went on to raise the subject of the ideas adopted but pending. 'It's all very well to have decided that an idea cannot be put into practice right away. But if it's going to be pending, could we have a date put beside it? Otherwise you might seem to be lacking a little in sincerity!'

I came away impressed by what the teams had achieved and by the management attitude. Even though there had been a breakdown in communication it was not intended to be a sign that management didn't care. Indeed the more I met with the Stena management team the more convinced I became that they would like the staff to join the team and help the company prosper in the difficult times ahead. But if they don't let people know that their ideas have been accepted, or don't set specific targets for implementation, much of the benefit will be lost.

Nobody can predict what the impact of the Tunnel will be when it has been open long enough to prove its reliability and competitiveness. But as we showed in the programme, the crew of the *Invicta* can create the most delightful experience for customers travelling across the Channel above the waves, and there is no way the Tunnel can compete with them in that area.

CHAPTER FIVE

A JOURNEY INTO THE PAST

your past is only
useful if it helps you live
a better present

As a manager I reached the pinnacle of my career as UK sales and marketing director of Carboloy, one of Britain's leading producers of engineering tools. Carboloy was owned by one of the world's great conglomerates, General Electric of America.

Although the group was split into hundreds of separate company units, GE took the view that the management style throughout should reflect the powerful GE business ethic. Companies had to have a clear and simple vision, had to set 'aggressive targets' for improving profitability, and were judged strictly according to their performance in relation to these goals. Those who succeeded were rewarded handsomely; those who fell short – for whatever reason – could expect little mercy.

The group chief executive, the legendary Jack Welch (now chief executive of the parent company), believed in leaving very little to chance. The company headquarters in Connecticut became the example of 'best practice' that the subsidiary companies were expected to follow. To keep everyone on their toes, top executives were generally posted to a job for only eighteen months, after which they would move on to a new challenge.

When I worked at Carboloy I was a great admirer of Jack Welch's style of leadership and toughness. He was, in many ways, an ideal that I hoped to aspire to. He was personally committed to the company, expected others to share that commitment, and took a no-nonsense approach to under performance, albeit defined in the company's terms. I felt that good managers had absolutely nothing to fear. They would make sure that those below them performed to the same high standards.

Ten years on, and my views on what constitutes good management have radically changed, due to my Japanese experiences. In Japan too the big corporations set targets, but more broadly based ones than those in the West, where the 'bean counters' seem to call the tune. The Japanese do not embrace the idea of keeping people on their toes through fear – they know that once people buy into the vision they will deliver and improve on company targets through the power of Kaizen and the operation of the team ethic. And the Japanese would certainly disagree profoundly with the philosophy of promoting senior managers according to the sort of formula they had at General Electric.

In all these matters I think the Japanese have got it right. Indeed, on reflection, my experience at GE illustrated the dangers of the 'new broom syndrome' which meant that the incoming executive would want to make the maximum possible visible impact and move on before – to mix metaphors – the chickens came home to roost.

Driving from Yorkshire to Peterborough in the Fen Country one Wednesday morning, these thoughts were uppermost in my mind. My next workshop was to be at Hotpoint Refrigeration, one of the last bastions of the British 'white goods' industry and now owned 50/50 by GEC (chief executive Lord Weinstock) and GE of America. When the company had been contacted about taking part in the series there had been immediate interest. They had already begun to implement a number of Japanese-inspired industrial practices and, it was felt, a TV programme showing how the workers were improving the quality of the refrigerators they produced could bring the company an advantage over the competition.

As I turned into the factory complex and checked in at the gate-house, I could see that Hotpoint was no mean enterprise. It was spread over a 38,000 square meter site, with offices to my right and the large sheds of the industrial complex, looking pretty spick and span, stretching away on my left.

I was particularly happy to include a company like this in the series. In the early sixties British companies had supplied 80 per cent of home demand in the growing market for washing machines, fridges, cookers and new-fangled ideas like dishwashers. Then we stalled. Italy, which had been only a small player after the war, piled in with cheap but reliable fridges; the Germans grabbed a large share of the washing machine market with models that were reliable and up-to-the-minute in sophisticated controls; and the French, the Dutch and the Swedes all upped their share. British manufacturers, on the whole, lost out. It was a tribute to Hotpoint that it had come through and survived as a major player.

If Hotpoint could survive the carnage of the eighties and learn how to be a world-class company, it could yet be a base from which to regrow a thriving British white goods industry – even if it was now 50 per cent American-owned.

I was shown into the office of the works director, Paul Lynch, a youngish man with a pleasant Irish accent and an obvious concern to keep Hotpoint ahead in the business. He put me in the picture about the troubles of the past and the challenge he now faced.

In the late sixties Hotpoint had been absorbed into the new industrial giant GEC as part of prime minister Harold Wilson's strategy to create a strong base for a competitive British manufacturing sector. The received wisdom of the time was 'big is beautiful'. Britain's main competitors seemed to have larger industrial companies than we had, so the creation of larger groupings seemed to make sense.

There is no question that over the years GEC has turned in good profits and generated cash reserves on a mighty scale – the celebrated 'cash mountain' that Arnold Weinstock kept in the bank because in the seventies and early eighties there appeared to be no chance of getting a bigger return from investing in the business. But, on the company's own admission, creating bigger units to serve the white goods market – through amalgamation and specialization – created a new set of problems. Chief among them were falling standards. Workers, not surprisingly, can find big complex companies impersonal and difficult to belong to. Quality, which depends so much on a close identification between workers and the company, tends to suffer as a result.

In 1973 Chaim Schreiber, a naturalized Briton who had made his name in office furniture, bought a share of Hotpoint and took over as chief executive. Schreiber was dedicated to changing the culture at Hotpoint, which in common with many large British factories had been plagued by 'them and us' attitudes. He started by abolishing the practice of clocking in (people were responsible and they could all tell the time, he argued) and introduced a profit-sharing scheme. This was accompanied by improved holiday pay. His idea was to make everybody proud of working for Hotpoint and more responsive to the need for better productivity and better quality. To this end, he also abolished piecework and upgraded the factory. As a result, so the company believed, Hotpoint would be transformed into a leading edge manufacturer that could hold its own with the best.

It was classic textbook stuff, and for a while the strategy seemed to pay off. The company was restored to profitability, the consumer boom of the late eighties led to a strong growth in the market for refrigerators and fridge freezers, and Hotpoint held its own with nearly 20 per cent of the UK market. But was Hotpoint improving fast enough to hold its own in a world where competitors were improving too? The onset of the 1990s brought a slump, followed by low-cost competition from an unexpected quarter. Turkey had become a new and dangerous player. 'The trouble is,' Paul Lynch informed me, 'they can sell the same capacity fridge at 15 per cent below our price.'

So, although Hotpoint currently still employed 1800 people at Peterborough (down from a peak of 11,000 in 1972), its future was by no means secure.

Paul Lynch was an interesting man – he had not risen to his present position through the conventional management graduate route but had come in as a graduate designer. After impressing the company with his ability to lead a team, he had won promotion from the Hotpoint washing machine factory in North Wales.

Possessed of a very firm grasp of the imperatives of modern manufacture, he wanted the company to be customer-focused, delivering the sort of quality in design, performance and reliability that the discriminating modern customer demanded. He also wanted to take waste of every sort out of the business to improve its cost structure. 'Lean production' was the aim, and he accepted that this would require a teamwork approach, allowing the people who did the job to work out better ways of doing it.

The more I heard about the company's approach, the more I wondered why they were finding things so difficult: they seemed well down the road in adopting world-class techniques. So I asked Paul what role he saw for me.

'We want you to get across the message that we really mean it when we say we want everyone to be involved. You can help do that for us.'

We got to talking about Jack Welch and his uncompromising search for better ways of doing things, and I told him of my years with GE at Carboloy. Did I imagine it, or did Paul Lynch seem slightly unnerved?

The first step was to hold a ninety-minute management conference. Hotpoint had come on board too late to send more than a token presence

A Journey into the Past

to the Manchester weekend briefing – although the productivity manager, Dave Christian, attended and made a solid contribution. To make up for this, the entire senior management team now assembled in the board room to hear of the thinking behind the exercise we were about to embark on. In the process, I wanted to take the opportunity to emphasize the new role of the manager and supervisor.

In preparing for the session I had spent some time in the training room, where I came across a document headed GE Management Values. It stressed 'Unyielding Integrity', 'Customer-focused Vision', setting and reaching 'Aggressive Targets', 'Relish[ing] Change', displaying 'Enormous Energy' – all vintage Jack Welch. But the values laid a new emphasis on 'hating bureaucracy', and having 'a passion for excellence', reflecting the new management-speak. Most remarkable of all were the exhortations: 'Have the Self-confidence to Empower Others...' and '[Be] Open to Ideas from Anywhere.' If this policy was being implemented here at Hotpoint, then all I could do was assist and accelerate it. Much of the document could have been written by me!

The management meeting briefing was the first and only one to be filmed. In place of the two-day course we had run in Manchester, I had compressed the basics into what I hoped would be an uplifting one-hour summary. The affair went well enough until I came to my definition of experts – the 'real experts' are the people who are trained and experienced in doing a particular job, the people whom we have to involve in improving the business. As a throw-away remark I rounded this off by observing that

in too many businesses the title of 'expert' was given to 'some smart-arsed young graduate straight out of college' who knew nothing about which direction we were trying to go in at the daily work level.

I caught sight of Paul Lynch's face: it was set in an undisguised scowl. From that moment on, I sensed a profound change of mood. Fewer people were willing to join in the banter, or openly to accept the truth of what I was saying.

'Well, gentlemen,' I wound up, 'have you any questions or reactions?'

Paul Lynch immediately raised my reference to 'smart-arsed' graduates. He had taken it to mean that I held *all* graduates in contempt. Most of the people sitting around the table were graduates.

I explained. My objection was only to 'smart-arsed' graduates – those who swaggered on to the shop-floor and disdained to acknowledge that experienced operatives had a much better understanding than they had of the specific processes involved. But, try as I might, I wasn't able to get the distinction across.

The heat that was raised in the ensuing discussion made me feel uneasy. I was trying to make a simple point that was fundamental to successful worker empowerment – yet the management team that had the task of promoting the policy wanted to argue about the role of graduates.

It is received wisdom that bringing graduates into industry will strengthen the organization. Far too many British graduates, we are told, go into the professions or the City when they would be better employed in manufacturing. I share that view. But that does not mean that a graduate manager should be treated as an all-knowing person who is better able than ordinary workers to improve specific parts of the business. Graduate managers need to learn a degree of humility. Graduates without practical experience – and that means the majority of them to begin with – are the products of an academic process. Their learning is theoretical rather than practical, intellectual rather than intuitive. In a manufacturing industry context, and probably in other contexts too, nothing beats direct, hands-on experience.

In Japan graduates are employed by all the great industrial corporations, but no one would take their advice on technical matters or let them loose to manage workgroups before they have been given practical training. It is one of the more attractive aspects of Japanese culture that graduate recruits show the utmost respect to the operators. In addition, managers tend to be moved regularly from department to department not to keep everyone on their toes, but to broaden their understanding of the business. The process also obliges them to seek advice and help from people who already work there. Sadly, that is not the approach I find in Britain, where young graduates not only demotivate the people they manage but often go on to screw the whole place up. What we need is a blend of intellectual and intuitive skills – our graduates and our shop-floor experts working together on equal terms – to produce the best results for the company.

By the time the management seminar drew to a close it was obvious that they hadn't been too impressed by the theory behind my workshops. They knew the workforce had to be mobilized to improve the business; they also knew that quality and improved performance depended on this. What they did not fully grasp was how to start the process.

'Gentlemen,' I said, 'you just go out and do it. That will be the lesson of the next two days.'

I had already made a tour of the Hotpoint works and looked at the area selected for immediate improvement. The factory was a large, sprawling affair, that manufactured a range of refrigerators and had its own design and development department. It also housed a top secret project – a new model intended to secure the company's future markets. This was hush-hush stuff that we weren't allowed to film.

The most striking feature of the building was the impressive-looking conveyor system which carried a stream of fridges in various stages of production. This, I was told, was a system installed by Mr Schreiber twenty years previously. It was a grand vision, but not as impressive as it looked. My mother used to say: 'Don't judge a man by the cut of his suit, but by the quality of the material.' There's a superficial attractiveness in having parts whizzing about all over the place, but as I looked at the conveyors moving up and across and down and around and along, I wondered, for all the time and motion involved, just how much value was being added to the product. ·

However, there were signs everywhere that some Japanese thinking had taken root: the factory looked clean with white lines marking off broad passageways; there were clearly designated positions for bins; and one department even had a notice-board complete with photographs of each member and notes on their birthdays and hobbies. Someone was trying hard to build a team spirit. Had I been a visiting director, or even a business journalist writing a background piece for the financial pages, I think I would have been impressed enough. But I suspect most journalists would have been steered away from the area that the Sid workshop was being asked to tackle – the press shop.

Presses, for those who are not familiar with manufacturing, are hefty pieces of equipment which bend and form metal into the desired shape. The speed at which the press shop operates can be absolutely critical for the whole production process. It is in effect churning out raw materials for the assembly process further down the line.

As it happens, press shops have a habit of being unreliable. Machines weighing as much as 100 tonnes have to cope with tremendous stresses as the giant pressing surfaces are raised and lowered. It was not unusual to find that two out of the four large presses at Hotpoint had broken down. But delays occur not only because of breakdowns. Every time the machines are switched from making one part to another they have to be stopped to allow the 'tools' to be changed and reset precisely in position. These dies are the very hard metal bending and cutting surfaces that are bolted on to the opposing jaws of the press. Changing from one set of tools to another, as I explained earlier in the book, can easily take several hours on a big press.

Although the press shop was old and seemed to have escaped the Schreiber treatment I was confident that the heroes who worked here could transform it almost overnight. I had seen places much worse than this utterly transformed by a confident workforce entrusted with a few simple Japanese techniques.

Pat McGee, an outwardly genial Scotsman, was responsible for the section's output and general management. He took a paternal interest in the men and women under his control and was very much in charge. His support for the cultural transformation we were about to embark on would be all-important.

DAY ONE

If there was a single lesson to be learnt from the Hotpoint workshop it was to demonstrate the gulf between the principles on which the company was supposed to be running and the actual situation on the ground. Nothing I had seen or heard before we met in the training centre had prepared me for the workshop reaction. Here was a company that had started to adopt Japanese techniques and the latest Jack Welch thinking on what constitutes a world-class business. To the casual observer, briefed beforehand on the Schreiber years and on the management strategy to implement new ways of working – tapping into the potential of the workforce – the factory looked set on the road to achieve that goal. To judge from the workers who took part in the workshop – and from a special briefing I gave to the night shift – the view from the shop-floor was entirely different.

The twenty-odd participants were overwhelmingly male and could have been drawn from a past era. They hated their work, they felt hemmed in by management restrictions, they distrusted the management's motives. Peterborough, a pleasant place set in the heart of rural England, was about the last place I would have expected to find such a distrust of management. Given the Schreiber policy and the new GE 'management values' it seemed almost inexplicable. What I had before me seemed to be a casebook example of the bloody-minded British worker of the sixties rather than his nineties' counterpart.

However, in my view the bloody-minded worker is always the product of the company environment. Outside the factory these twisted souls can be dependable friends, caring parents, supportive husbands – the salt of the earth. Within the first two hours of the workshop it became clear why they were bloody-minded.

For a start, there was bitter resentment about what was seen as management's bad planning in relation to output. When orders had fallen the previous spring, they complained that the factory had been laid off for a week. On their return to work, things had changed so dramatically that they had been asked to work overtime to catch up: this had created a very bad impression of management's ability to handle production scheduling. The workforce also resented the style of supervision: Pat McGee was hardly a popular figure, accused of always being on their back and making work an unpleasant experience. As for the new company policy of giving responsibility to the workers for improving quality and performance, they had never heard of it. Even a well-intentioned management initiative to generate more ideas from the workforce by holding a competition and awarding prizes for the best had misfired. It was seen as a poor substitute for a previous policy of paying cash bonuses for ideas that were adopted. This was a very unhappy bunch of people.

The only way to win them round was to create a vision that they could buy into. I began by describing two invisible 'beams' at the factory gate. When I explained that as they arrived at work one beam took their brain out of their heads and the other, more importantly, took their hearts out of their bodies, I detected the beginnings of a breakthrough. Most companies have these beams across their entrances, and turning them off is the first step towards creating our new environment. If we could create a workplace where people were respected and were allowed to make their contribution to the success of the company, would they go along with it? Just as I have found with every group of British workers I have ever worked with, they indicated that they would be only too happy to buy in to this simple vision.

By lunchtime the objectives of the workshop were already taking shape. We would tackle change-over time on the larger presses, speed up the work on the small ones, and try to rebuild pride in the workplace by completely cleaning up one of the largest presses. After the aggravation of the morning session, the show was on the road.

People often wonder how it is possible to teach three quite different techniques in the course of a single afternoon, dealing with people, many of whom have had little education in the formal sense. The answer is threefold.

Firstly, all the techniques share one element of Japanese problem-solving – the problem-and-solution chart often referred to as the fishbone or Ishikawa diagram. The principle of the chart is very simple. All our visible problems are caused by our real problems, which are often hidden. If when using our real experts we can identify all the causes of our problems, and cure them, we will automatically 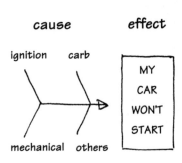 cure the visible effect of these problems. An example is when our car breaks down. The problem may appear to be that our car won't start, but the real problem is dirty plugs, no petrol, or one or more of many other possibilities. If we cure all of these problems, our car will start. We must then make sure that all the actions we took become standard procedure (keep our car serviced and filled up) so that the problem cannot arise again.

Secondly, we must tap into people's intuitive knowledge not on an individual basis but on a team basis – a team of equals in which there are no leaders and in which nothing but positive thinking is tolerated. We know that when eleven men take the field in a football cup-tie they believe victory can only come as a team effort. Then somehow being part of the team makes everybody try harder, so as not to let their team-mates down.

But most important of all is the third factor. We must tap into the passion of the human heart, a reservoir of potentially huge commitment that everybody has inside them but which lies dormant until released by a skilful leader.

Sun T'su wrote 2300 years ago about the immense advantages that moral commitment gave to any army. People who feel they are fighting for a noble cause will achieve miracles. For most workers is there a more noble cause than the survival of their jobs, upon which their livelihood and that of their families depend? If workers feel that change will threaten their jobs, their wholehearted cooperation cannot be expected; but if change protects jobs by making the company stronger, by helping the company defeat the threatening enemy, then the hearts of the workforce can be counted on to win the battle.

This is a truth that Japanese employers recognized long ago. We in the West cannot afford to ignore that lesson.

By the end of Day One I had the Hotpoint workshop teams raring to go, and trained on the techniques to use. We were using a mixture of techniques, similar to those we used at Videoprint and Lambert Howarth – workpiece flow analysis and 5 S housekeeping, with the addition of set-up time reduction. We were going to demonstrate to management that the expertise of the teams was a powerful force that they could not ignore.

Day Two

One of the interesting features of making the television series was the fact that I was never told which of the team members were being filmed outside the workplace to show the way that attitudes could so easily be changed given the right management approach. At Hotpoint the production team had selected three: a gentle but outspoken amateur gardener called Aubrey Keen; a cheerful, solid operator called Harry Lewis who was a keen bird-watcher; and Darrin Brown, who was in his twenties and a keen footballer for a local amateur club. They shared a distaste for their jobs and strong feelings about how they were treated at work. No one seemed to think they had any role to play apart from bringing a pair of 'hands' to service the company. Work belittled them. To all three life was out there beyond the factory gates. They couldn't wait for the working day to finish. Each of the three was in a separate team when we began the second day of the workshop – the day when things really begin to hum.

Darrin's team were aiming to reduce by at least half the fifty-three minutes it took to change over one of the big presses. They had to do so without spending any money and without using any extra people. It may not sound exciting, but 'set-up time reduction' was one of the key techniques developed by Shigeo Shingo when he worked as consultant engineer for Toyota in the 1960s. Shingo saw that the key to beating the competition was to deliver customers what they wanted, when they wanted it, and at a lower cost than other firms. He was involved in developing set-up time reduction, a key component of the Toyota production system. Let me explain, using a simplified model factory to put the point across.

In the sixties large American corporations mass-produced cars in long production runs. Let us say that in one factory they turned out 5000 cars of the same specification each week. At the weekend the tool-setters – skilled craftsmen – moved in to change over the machine tools to produce 5000 of a different model in week two. And so on for a five-week period....

That system was all very well as long as customers ordered each of the five models in roughly the same amounts, and were prepared to wait up to five weeks for delivery. If they didn't behave in this ideal way, it created a problem

for the manufacturer. At that time it could take an entire day to change over production, and it would be highly costly to close down the factory in mid-week to do the job.

But suppose the change-over could be reduced from ten hours to, say, ten minutes? Then the factory could switch production as and when it needed to, and meet customers' orders exactly as soon as they came in. As a bonus, factories would no longer be producing cars in great batches. That would reduce stock costs and reduce defects in the production – bored workers working on long runs make more mistakes.

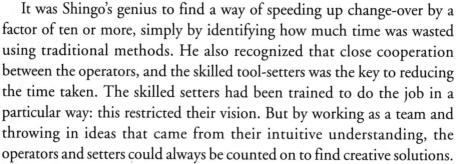

It was Shingo's genius to find a way of speeding up change-over by a factor of ten or more, simply by identifying how much time was wasted using traditional methods. He also recognized that close cooperation between the operators, and the skilled tool-setters was the key to reducing the time taken. The skilled setters had been trained to do the job in a particular way: this restricted their vision. But by working as a team and throwing in ideas that came from their intuitive understanding, the operators and setters could always be counted on to find creative solutions. Shingo developed a way of analyzing each step in the process to see whether it was strictly necessary or could be speeded up. We should treat our machinery like Formula 1 racing cars during a pitstop. When the car arrives, everything is there ready and waiting and all the unnecessary activity is eliminated during the car's time in the pit. It was this system that I passed on to the Hotpoint team.

Darrin Brown was one of the keenest members of the group, and obviously bright and energetic. But he was not the most effective member of the team. In Britain we don't take easily to the notion that ideas should flow out of a group and be written down before considering whether they will work or not. If we take the Zen approach, we must let the ideas flow; and the easiest way to stop the flow is to criticize an idea as it emerges. If people keep telling you your ideas are rubbish you are not going to risk putting them up to be shot at. As so often happens, it was not the apparently bright people who made the biggest contribution to Darrin's group. Again that is one reason why this approach turns people into heroes. They discover a magic within themselves that they did not know they had.

By early afternoon the change-over team were well on their way to hitting their target. Just to prove that their ideas worked, they were timing the setter as he did it their way.

The second group was not, however, having such an easy time. Aubrey Keen and his colleagues in that team had set themselves the job of speeding up production by 25 per cent by making the work easier and more fun. They had chosen to work on one of the smaller presses, usually worked by Tonia House, also a member of the team.

Tonia worked the press as she normally did, while the others timed all the operations and considered how to speed them up. With little prompting from me, they came up with the idea of feeding the parts into the press and removing the finished pressing through using the force of gravity and a couple of metal chutes made from bending pieces of scrap aluminium. A further refinement was to raise the power pedal on to a box so that she could reach it easily while she was doing the job. All the stretching and bending that had been making her life a misery were eliminated at a stroke.

There was only one snag. The safety officer, one of the shop managers, was reluctant to let the change take place. The metal chutes protruded through the bars of the safety cage that surrounded the machine. If it had not been for the presence of the TV cameras I very much doubt if the improvement would have been made. Yet when the team measured the productivity of the new system it was 28 per cent faster than the old one, and the operator was completely safe.

The third team, which included Harry Lewis, had set out to clean up a giant press and make it something they could all be proud of by painting and polishing it. They faced the biggest problems of any team. They also uncovered some strong evidence of the nature of the existing company culture.

The aim of the exercise was not merely to restore pride in people's work, important though that was. One of the recurrent problems in the press shop was the unreliability of the big presses; cleaning up the machine made it easier to spot tell-tale signs of wear and tear – things that could easily be put right before a total breakdown took place.

(Again, although the Japanese can teach us all a lesson about the benefits of a clean and tidy factory, the basic principle was known to my mother and grandmother long ago: cleanliness is next to godliness and a stitch in time saves nine.)

To have the machine ready for inspection was a mammoth job, but it was tackled with energy and good cheer. Michael Soccio, from the sizeable Peterborough Italian community, was so enthused by the project that the cameras recorded him singing 'O Sole Mio' in a fine tenor voice!

By midday it was obvious that the muck of decades was not going to give way to mere elbow grease. The team reckoned they needed a steam cleaner and knew that there was one available in the stores. The supervisor, Pat McGee, and other managers had been looking on. The team was told that the steam cleaner was not available. It was only after our short lunch break that I heard of the controversy.

Relying on the fact that I had the backing of Paul Lynch and the senior managers, I walked to the stores, found a portable steam cleaner lying idle, and had it brought along to the press shop. Not everybody was pleased to see it arrive. However by four o'clock Harry Lewis and his fellow team members were putting the finishing touches to the job. The machine looked like new, the faces beamed with pride, and top management at least was impressed.

They should have been equally impressed by the outcome of the change-over project: previous time 53 minutes; new time 25 minutes. The workers had achieved an improvement of over 50 per cent in a single day!

Ten weeks later we came back to Hotpoint to see if the progress had been maintained. Superficially it had, with four large presses cleaned up and painted and the whole area looking much tidier. But my worry about Hotpoint was that there were people in middle management who felt threatened by the whole process and who were in a position to destroy the whole initiative. And to some extent that seemed to have happened.

It transpired that almost all the visible improvement had taken place in the week before our return, during a 'lay-off' week. (The refrigeration business is seasonal, with a falling off in demand in late summer; to cope with these fluctuations Hotpoint works a system of annualized hours, with more time off at this time of year.) When I raised the matter with Pat McGee he felt it was a perfectly good way to use slack time.

More serious was the complaint that it had taken weeks to have the aluminium chutes produced for the smaller presses, and that the design did not conform to the cardboard template sent to the design department by the team. There was a general complaint that the design engineers, the cost department, and the production engineers were dragging their feet over the changes the teams wanted to see. All these represented middle levels of management – people in a position to stop things happening if they had a mind to.

Faced with this sort of resistance to change, the heroes I release need to have the support of top management. At Hotpoint Paul Lynch certainly seemed keen to press ahead with continuous improvement in the Japanese way, but he will need real guts to see the changes through.

So what are the general lessons of the Hotpoint workshops?

First, I think I can say I was truly astonished at the gulf between what management thought they had achieved in the journey towards empowerment and the workers' own perception. The people who worked in the press shop were concerned about the way the company was being managed, and deeply distrusted the management line – all this despite the reforms made by Chaim Schreiber in the seventies. The situation at Hotpoint supports my view that it is necessary for managements to go more than halfway to meet the workers if they are to win their confidence.

At Hotpoint, as elsewhere in Britain, there was an enduring sense of insecurity that haunted the workforce and made change difficult to accept. The senseless policies of treating people as merely a factor in production, like raw materials and marketing, have taken their toll. People have brains and hearts to give to the cause of the company in return for being treated with respect and fairness: brains and hearts are what companies need now to succeed.

However, if the Hotpoint experience emphasized anything, it was the severe problems of reforming middle management. If we are to release the talents of our people it can only be by giving them the necessary tools and letting them get on with improving the way the job is done by making it easier, faster, safer and more fun. This faces middle managers with considerable challenges. First of all they have to accept that, when it comes to doing the actual work, it is the operators and not they who are the experts. This is true even when middle managers have been highly skilled operators themselves.

In the case of Pat McGee, we had just that situation. He was a timeserved craftsman with years of experience in press shop work, who clearly felt it was his duty to supervise people closely to maintain the sort of standards he wanted. He apparently did not grasp the fact that, by constantly being seen metaphorically gazing over the shoulder of his workers, he was depriving them of initiative, responsibility and ultimately job satisfaction.

The lesson from Japan is that, by giving people responsibility and creating a team ethic, it is also possible to improve ways of working *continuously*. This is something that no supervisor, no matter how skilled, can possibly do.

So what should be the role of someone like Pat McGee? As I said before, the managers are there to 'support' the workers, but what exactly does that mean? To explain this new role to the supervisor, I tell my horse-riding story.

Some years ago I was on holiday with some friends in South Wales, and we decided to go pony trekking. I had never been on a horse before, so it was with some concern that I climbed aboard a huge creature (it looked more like an elephant without a trunk) at the riding stables.

We set off, and to my surprise I discovered that I was a natural horseman. As I sat there doing my John Wayne impression, it all seemed so simple. If our leader went left, I made the horse go left; if she stopped, I made my horse stop. The horse was fully under my control, wasn't it?

After about two miles of turning and twisting along coastal paths — a feat of horsemanship that Harvey Smith (or for that matter Harvey Jones) would have been proud of – a thought occurred to me. I released the reins and sat there motionless: just as I had suspected, the horse was doing all the work. All my tugging with the reins and pressing with my legs and pretending to be in charge was contributing nothing to the process – it was just making the horse's task more difficult and his life more miserable. After this discovery, I just sat back and enjoyed the journey.

This little story illustrates clearly the new role of leaders. They must set the direction so that their people know where they are going, supply them with the tools and training they will need, and ensure that they have feedback on what they are achieving. Then the leaders must get out of the way and let the people get on with it.

I still believe that Britain can rebuild its position as a manufacturing nation and that companies like Hotpoint can become world-beaters. The workers who attended the workshop, as the television programmes showed, were

in our new world 'star managers' make their people shine

people of character and ingenuity. All companies have such people. We simply need to work harder to release them from their chains.

For two days we did that job at Peterborough. The nightmare is that we did not release them, but simply slackened the chains for a bit. As the workers go charging off in search of better ways of working, the chain can suddenly go tight again and yank their heads off. But if the Hotpoint managers adopt the role model shown below, I am sure this will not happen.

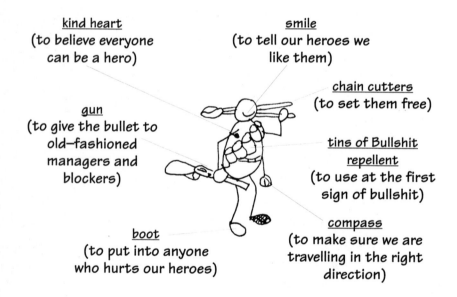

kind heart
(to believe everyone
can be a hero)

smile
(to tell our heroes we
like them)

chain cutters
(to set them free)

gun
(to give the bullet to
old–fashioned
managers and
blockers)

tins of Bullshit
repellent
(to use at the first
sign of bullshit)

boot
(to put into anyone
who hurts our heroes)

compass
(to make sure we are
travelling in the right
direction)

CHAPTER SIX

THE HEALTH FACTORY

When I went to that first production meeting in the offices of Lauderdale Productions, I was asked if I would mind searching for heroes in a hospital rather than a factory.

'A hospital? That's a neat idea. We can look at a hospital as a caring place, which it should be, but we could just as well look at it as a factory that produces well people.'

I hadn't thought about hospitals in that way before, but of course the definition was spot on. In the world I am trying to create, every workplace would be a caring place. Even so, the caring factory is at the moment a bit of a curiosity; the fact that hospitals attract caring people gives them a head start. Just as the best Japanese-style factory aims to delight the customer with prompt delivery of a quality product at the lowest possible price, hospitals can delight their ultimate customers, the community, by delivering to patients the most efficient service, to the highest standard, within the budgets that we as a community can afford.

That may sound very much like the language of the present Health Service managers and indeed of Virginia Bottomley herself. Where I differ is on the style of management needed to achieve the goals. Too many British managers are wedded to the balance sheet; are fascinated by 'systems' designed to deliver results, but which generate paperwork instead; and don't appear to know how to release the talents of ordinary workers inside the organization, who are the key to success. As far as I could judge, the new 'market-oriented' Health Service was being driven by smart young managers who carried a balance sheet in one hand and a BS5750 manual in the other. I was concerned about the effect they would be having on morale and motivation.

I had never actually worked in a hospital before, but using the yardstick of BCS (Basic Common Sense), there would be heroes in any hospital just waiting to be freed from their chains. I have yet to find an organization that didn't have them, and a factory for making 'well people' would be no different. Of course, I had very little idea of what a hospital workshop would look at. But I lost no sleep over it: when I got there the ways and means would, as usual, simply suggest themselves. Conventional consultants go in and research the institution and its problems, then analyze their findings, then come up with solutions, but I don't. You might say that such an 'intellectual' approach is akin to looking at a problem through the panes of a stained-glass window (the stained glass being the intellectual colours of the consultants' opinion). My approach is to hold only plain glass in front of the problem and let the truth pour through it.

A few weeks later I met Michael Emberton for the first time. Michael was the recently appointed chairman of the Countess of Chester Hospital Trust, and he was attending the *Sid's Heroes* management weekend seminar in Manchester.

Hospital trusts currently have a central role to play in a government strategy that aims to bring better cost control and better management of resources to the Health Service. In the long term the idea is that each hospital trust will sell its services to family doctors and local health authorities, whose funds in turn will come mainly from the public purse. If the trust hospitals don't run themselves efficiently, or fail to produce a good-quality service, then they will simply go out of business. That at least is the theory of the 'internal market'.

It is a truism that hospitals in possession of these new business principles must be in need of people with business experience to run them. That was where Michael Emberton came in. He had had a long career in business on Merseyside, been appointed chairman of the Mersey-side Health Authority and now, at the request of the Health Secretary, been appointed part-time chairman of the Countess of Chester Trust.

To give him his due, in the course of the two-day seminar he grew more and more enthusiastic over the idea of having me in to find and release the talents of the staff. The Hospital Trust had already begun preparing for the government Investors in People scheme, which has admirable aims expressed in the language of involvement, participation and training. Fine language doesn't add up to delivering the goods, but Michael's obvious sincerity in his desire to build a team spirit to deliver a good service made me warm to him.

However, Michael may not have been entirely his own man. At Manchester he was accompanied by his chief executive, Paul Barrow. Paul must be typical of the new breed of full-time Health Service managers, trained to think corporately, sold on the idea of using the latest business system to achieve results. I classed him as a numbers man – someone who put faith in financial outcomes, who could read a balance sheet with the best of them and by this method root out inefficiency and waste.

Of course everybody in business has to be aware of cost. The real question is how we go about keeping costs down or reducing them. In a business as heavily labour-intensive as health care, the easy option is labour shedding. But while this can achieve short-term results, the remaining workers are hardly likely to engage in the process of continuous improvement that would produce far larger savings over the longer period.

I believe the effects of using staff in a positive way to improve performance can be even more dramatic in a hospital than in industry. Patients will surely recover more quickly when they are cared for by staff who themselves feel cared for.

Before taking on a business assignment, you will recall that I normally have to convince myself that the top management looks on the workforce as its most precious asset and is prepared to treat them with tender loving care. In all honesty, although he was a decent man, these were not vibes I got from Paul Barrow. When I stressed the absolute necessity of guaranteeing that there would be no redundancies as a result of any changes that the 'heroes' might make, he looked uncomfortable. Did he know something I didn't?

Still, in April I found myself driving through Chester on my way to visit the hospital for the first time, excited by the challenge. I was to have a briefing from Mike Emberton and Paul Barrow and see around the hospital.

The very name 'Countess of Chester Hospital' had conjured up an image of a large Victorian institution, but it proved not to be like that at all. The main building was very modern, with a grand reception area and wide corridors leading off to the wards, operating theatres and specialist treatment units (the hospital was very proud of its new scanner and felt it would give the Countess of Chester an advantage in the new marketplace).

By any standards this was a big business, employing 2300 staff and handling an annual budget of £47 million. In the course of a year the hospital cared for 48,000 inpatients and about 250,000 outpatients. I thought of all those people working on such a huge complex. The challenge for management was to keep them motivated and preserve a sense that this was just one big happy family. If they could do that, and use these people to drive the improvements inside the business, then both patients and taxpayers could reap the benefit.

From the front of the building, sweeping over the road with an architectural flourish, ran a new bridge that linked the main building with the clinic block and maternity unit on the other side. If the whole hospital complex had been on just these two sites then the management task would have been demanding enough. But many of the beds and facilities were housed in the old Chester Royal Infirmary building over a mile away.

The bridge itself gave me my first inkling into the problems that were to lie ahead. It meant the main buildings and the clinic and maternity blocks could now be reached without crossing the road and risking the elements. But to cross it meant mounting a steep ramp. I was introduced to some of the hospital porters who had to use it and it seemed the gradient was so steep that taking a heavy meal trolley across it required great effort. I had to sympathize. And it wasn't only food; trolleys carrying

patients came this way too. Although I am sure there are safety devices on the trolleys, I imagined that a runaway trolley here could be an unpleasant experience.

The managers probably considered the bridge a great improvement on what had gone before, and in some ways it probably was. But its unpopularity among the hospital porters told me one thing for sure: these were people who felt left out of the decision-making process and risked becoming alienated.

The briefing with Michael Emberton helped to fill in the overall picture. Paul Barrow was in charge of an ambitious strategy that saw the Countess of Chester eventually coalescing on a single site to become the most important general hospital immediately south of the Mersey. However, that lay in the future. In the short term the Trust was under great pressure to eliminate its deficit (standing at £700,000) and to implement a policy (coming from the Department of Health) of putting 'non-core' portering and housekeeping services out to tender.

Of course, if you are an accountant concerned only with the immediate numbers, such a policy makes good sense. The lowest tender will very likely come from an outside firm that may know a lot about cleaning or shoving trolleys uphill but not very much about a hospital. But even if the new people are enthusiastic cleaners and carriers – and in my experience they are not – policies like this undermine the whole culture of total involvement and continuous improvement that any business worth its salt should want to build up. Such a policy undermines trust in management among the staff that are kept in-house (they worry, will it be me next?), and of course it poses the enormous problem of blending into the workplace teams the outsiders who are seen to have taken other workers' jobs. Then there's the problem of differing management philosophies. As you will now understand, teamwork depends on a radical rethink of the traditional management role – out goes command and control, in comes supportive management. But when work goes out to tender it is very difficult to guarantee that the firms taking the jobs will share that ethos.

The idea of 'downsizing' by hiving off non-core activity is a nonsense that has become orthodoxy in Britain. Imagine having in the hospital an obese patient who has to lose weight as a matter of urgency. One solution would be to chop off a leg. The fact that the patient loses the power to walk would seem to rule that out. Yet managers gaily cut off 'limbs' as part of a short-term balance sheet approach.

The way for the fat man to lose weight is for him to become fitter. Then he will be not only healthy but able to play a full role in society. To make a company fit we have to make all the limbs work more effectively, without ever forgetting that they belong to a single body.

In Japan there are 'core' workers and others who operate 'flexible' contracts – in any business where there is an ebb and flow of work such a system can be justified. (Hotpoint's 'annualized hours' scheme is, however, a better alternative.) But successful Japanese companies would baulk at sacking workers and then putting their work out to 'lowest bidder' outsiders (even during the severe 1992–4 recession Japanese firms kept up employment levels wherever they could, despite all the predictions to the contrary made by the Western business gurus).

But here at Chester all was not lost. I learned that for the moment the plan to put out the porters' work had been shelved. However, it was not a good omen for the workshop. The very threat of doing it would have soured relations between workers and management, especially since there had been not too subtle hints that the only way to avoid 'contracting out' was for porters to accept longer hours with no increase in pay.

I returned in mid-May to run the workshop, still uneasy about the threatened contracting out. But I had decided that one way to see off the threat would be to use the workshop itself as part of the argument. It would convince managers that TLC (Tender Loving Care) policies towards the workforce would pay off in better patient care, more efficiency and lower costs. Once convinced, it would be up to them to take the evidence to the Health Secretary herself if need be. I hoped that Michael Emberton would take on that task.

DAY ONE

Early next morning I met the workshop teams for the first time. We gathered in an empty ward (there had been some ward closures in the hospital, although there were long-term plans to increase bed numbers) and I was immediately struck by what wonderful people they seemed to be. The team members, drawn from across the hospital departments, ranged from drivers through secretaries, nurses, ward sisters and receptionists, and even included a doctor.

After a flourish of the Bullshit Repellent (to ward off the spirit of the management 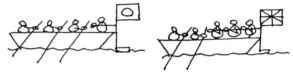 consultants which I felt hung over places like this!) I kicked off with my vision of a boat-race between a Japanese team and a British team. The Japanese team had three people rowing and one cox to steer. The British boat had two people rowing and three coxes steering. After the first race, which the Japanese won by a mile, the British team managers got together and decided they had lost because they had too few coxes! With just one person rowing this  time they raced again – and got beaten by two miles.

This raised a laugh, and then it all began to come out. This was a place where people generally wanted to work together to serve the patients but the new management structure seemed to get in the way. There were complaints of too much paper-shuffling, of too many layers of management that seemed to do nothing to add value to the business that the hospital should be in – caring for patients. The teams had detected a passion for new management fads like 'multi-skilling', which was being implemented without testing whether it was appropriate, and so on and so forth. Patient care was bound to suffer.

I had expected a reaction of this type. Whether the criticisms were fair or not, the new management systems seemed to be reinforcing the 'them and us' divide rather than dissolving it. Paul Barrow had told us earlier that he believed in good communications, but his description of the approach made it seem more than a little suspect. 'It works in a pyramid structure. I tell a group of people, they tell the staff, and so on.' He admitted it was not a two-way thing.

His approach to 'teamwork' was also rather puzzling. The hospital had invested in something called 'management teamwork training'. I had glanced at the paperwork and it seemed a classic piece of textbook nonsense, a paper-heavy procedure that would need extra management effort just to manage the paperwork! In any case teamwork training for management is a wrong-headed idea. Management should be part of the same team as the staff. Formalizing training of this type only reinforces the 'them and us' divide.

'Well,' I now said to the assembled teams, 'we need to have a different concept of what management is all about.' I drew them my upturned pyramid. 'That is how it is here – no?'

No reply. Then Mark Belham, a young doctor, reacted with a rhetorical question. 'I trust you will be trying to turn the pyramid round?'

There was a touch of cynical laughter.

Now I accept that when you get a group of Health Service professionals together they invariably have a negative view of the new management in the Health Service. Of course in the old days there were no 'professional managers' in the sense that we have them now. Somebody, somewhere, within the hospital has lost power as a result (usually the consultants) and there's bound to be some resentment. But Health Service managers are fooling themselves if they think that is the only explanation.

I can sympathize with new management teams inside the Health Service trying to put into practice some of the new business practices urged upon them by this consultant or that. But the danger is that in trying to change the culture of the Health Service from the top down is they only make matters worse. Over the two days of the workshop I came across plenty of evidence that command and control management is alive and well in the new business oriented Health Service.

On the other hand, I also grew more and more convinced that any health trust that could tap into the enthusiasm and caring instincts of the staff was on to a winner. At all the other companies I had visited so far as part of the TV series the workshop had begun with a line-up of faces that ran from suspicious through deeply cynical to downright hostile. Here at Chester there was very little of that. People had complaints to make, yes. But from the start there was a sense of common purpose: we are all here to make it better for the patients, to improve the service, to show that we care. What an enormous asset – it's a pity that so many NHS trusts seem unable to capitalize on it.

Now that we had broken the ice we had to consider the task before us. Michael Emberton had remarked early on that the hospital had a problem that was proving hard to crack. In a nutshell it was an administrative headache that was proving inconvenient and perhaps even dangerous for patients, irritating for doctors and other medical staff, and embarrassing for the hospital. Patients' records were going missing at the rate of sixty a week! People would turn up for an appointment at outpatients and be forced to wait while a search was made for their records.

Clare Blackwell, a lively sister from the orthopaedic clinic at the old Chester Royal, put it most clearly: 'It doesn't inspire confidence when you go to a hospital for an appointment and they seem to know nothing about you. One morning recently we had three patients we'd had no case sheets for. I had to speak to all of them, apologize for the delays, and try to explain the reason. I felt utterly deflated.'

There were plenty of theories on why the records were lost – too many hospital buildings, too much transporting, too much hoarding by doctors and their secretaries, a filing system that wasn't good enough. Whatever the cause, the loss of hospital records created inefficiency and extra costs as staff spent time on the telephone – time that should have been spent providing a better service to patients – playing a grotesque 'hunt the record' game. Even worse, perhaps, was the effect on staff morale and team spirit within the hospital.

Recrimination was the name of the game. Doctors blamed porters, receptionists blamed the Records Office, and the Records Office blamed the doctors. Debbie Blenkinsop, who worked in the Records Office, had

had enough: 'If you've not got the notes the consultants complain, the receptionists get it from the patients because the notes aren't there, and we get the blame all the time.'

Top management knew this was a big problem but had so far failed to find a solution. They were looking forward to the day when all records would be put on computers and couldn't be lost (a lot of managers make the mistake of thinking that computers are the answer to their prayers – they'll learn!). Until then they could at least console themselves with the thought that lost (or mislaid) records are a problem right across the Health Service. Of course the staff cared about the problem and there had even been efforts on the part of some areas, such as the orthopaedic clinic, to sort out the mess. But the statistics spoke for themselves.

So I saw here a golden opportunity to demonstrate that the problem could be solved if you put it in the hands of the real experts, the people who through their daily experience had an intuitive understanding of how the hospital functioned and how it could be improved. I had before me a fine mix of experts: twenty people drawn from five separate areas – medical care, transport, porterage, secretarial, reception and, of course, records itself. If I mixed them together in problem solving teams – some would call them project teams – we would produce results that would amaze the management, no doubt about that.

But what techniques should we use? The flow of records through the hospital was very similar to the flow of parts through a factory. It involved storage, transport, processing, transport and storage just like the materials being made up into shoes at Rawtenstall. So I started by teaching the system used to cut out Muda or waste on the factory floor (see page 180-182). The teams would then be asked to 'walk the job' and collect the facts at each stage. Then they would bring these back to be placed on a continuous improvement diagram (see page 187), after which they would identify the possible improvements, establishing as many as they could before putting them to the test.

Thus prepared, I was ready to unleash the teams. I gave them only my customary words of advice. They could do and have anything they wanted to improve the system, provided it did not require either more money or more people. Very reasonable, I quipped. But they took the point.

why is necessity the mother of invention?

Each of the teams chose to examine one small part of the problem. I like to refer to this breaking down of a problem into small parts as 'eating the elephant'.

With apologies to elephant lovers, if you tried to eat an elephant by yourself it could not be done all in one go. The sheer size of the meal would be off-putting and you would get indigestion long before it was completed quite apart from being unable to distinguish between, say, the strong meat of the thigh and the delicate flesh of the kidney. But if you take a group of people and chop up the elephant into bite-sized lumps, then it can be eaten and digested easily and its true nature understood. So each of the teams chose a section of the elephant/problem and started dividing it into manageable portions. This is another key concept behind the principle of continuous improvement.

One group went to the Records Office to see how the records were stored and to collect all the relevant facts. Finding piles of patient record files stored in supermarket trolleys was a bit of a shock. Finding and retrieving them when they were needed would be one hell of a problem.

There was plenty of evidence that the system was not working in other ways. Janet Capper, a consultant's secretary, picked up a 'tracer card' used to keep a track of patients' files and read the last entry. 'Look at this. This is a tracer card booked out to Ellesmere Port Hospital [another local hospital] to a Mr Haddad on 19 February 1992, which is over two years ago.' The record had never come back. Trying to recover cards like this under the present system was one of her personal nightmares. 'You have to ring Medical Records at Ellesmere Port and ask them if they've still got them, and if they haven't you have to find out where they've gone to. You then phone the next place... you're not a secretary but a detective.' It was certainly an eye-opener to Mark Belham, the doctor, who was seeing all this for the first time. 'That's NHS efficiency,' he remarked.

But uncovering the facts, using the dynamics of the problem-solving team, doesn't lead to the hand-wringing, sympathy and friction we normally have. This is because uncovering problems using the disciplined methodology of the continuous improvement diagram leads on to their active solution. Energy comes from deep down inside people and transforms them. Chris Mayers, the porter in the team, metaphorically rolled up his sleeves and got down to business: 'That's it, and the ball starts rolling here.' After that, there was no stopping them.

Despite this good start the human ego, especially the male ego, can often be a problem when the teams start off. Those who are used to being considered experts start to sound off and get in the way of the process. That's why I'm fond of telling them that when it comes to communication  God sent us a message in the way he designed our heads. He gave us two ears and one mouth, and only the mouth can be closed. Unfortunately, in my experience many managers and technicians do not seem to have understood what God meant. His simple message was: listen more than you talk. Too often I find we reverse this rule.

In the first information-gathering phase, listening to what people have to say is far more important than telling people what you think. Fortunately, in the Chester hospital people's egos were kept under control. This was surprising when you consider that, in the workshop, we were cocking a snook at traditional hierarchies and giving as much weight to the porter's opinion as to that of the doctor! It is natural for those who feel they have lost status to try and compensate by talking far too much, a tendency I always try to smother at birth.

Elsewhere in the hospital, the team which was looking at the transporting of the records had listed all the points where the system seemed to break down. The sorting bags were not properly labelled, which made mistakes inevitable; the van service between the hospitals did not match the needs of the consulting departments and often did not run on time, throwing surgeries into confusion. In addition, people all over the hospital felt no responsibility if records went astray – they could always blame it on someone else.

Now I daresay managers could have gone through the same process and come to much the same conclusions, but they would inevitably have ended up issuing memos telling people how to improve it. Through first-hand learning by doing it themselves, the people on the workshop were acquiring ownership of the process. In fact, as I walked round observing the teams in action it seemed perfectly obvious that these people were managing themselves far better than any manager could ever do. Yet we insist on believing that the 'I'll-tell-you-what-to-do' style of management makes sense.

Emboldened by the process, one of the teams decided to pay a visit on Steve Turner, the manager in charge of transport and porterage. They knocked on his door, marched into his office and asked for changes in the delivery van schedules. They wanted a 5.30 p.m. run to pick up records from the central store and deliver them to the clinic for an early morning start the next day. One of the team members was the nursing sister, Clare Blackwell, who came out triumphant: 'He was so uncomfortable he just agreed to everything.' It was perhaps a bit unfair on Steve; with the camera there he felt put on the spot.

But it was the reaction of another member of the team that I found more revealing. Brian Farley, the porter, confessed that he had never before had the opportunity to put his point to Steve Turner: 'If I don't get anything else out of today I've got that out of it.' Big institutions are, of course, notorious for creating an unhelpful distancing between staff and management. The hospital employed over two thousand people and it was impossible for top executives to have cosy chats with all of them. But at middle management level it should have been the aim to break the organization down into manageable, two-way communicating units, small enough to allow everybody a sense of belonging. Ten or twelve is about as big as we need go: soccer teams have eleven, rugby union teams are stretching it a bit at fifteen, rugby league at thirteen is better – but as a Yorkshireman I would say that! Was it not a sad commentary on the British way of doing business that Brian had never had a chance to communicate with his boss in this way before? But now that he had, he felt he was on a new path.

As the teams swept through the corridors at Chester, the tide of information-gathering was almost tangibly breaking down barriers that had grown up, and then defied all management efforts to eliminate them. In talking to the members of staff I had been struck by the fact that the hospital was a house divided against itself. Consultants and their secretaries were seen as stand-offish, porters were people who turned up late and gave a poor service, the receptionists lived in fear of the doctors, the records department in fear of almost everyone. Any business, even a small one, can become gripped by this sort of internal politics – a process of shifting blame on to someone else. Large organizations like hospitals can be especially prone to it. Yet over the two days of the workshop the walls dividing department from department began to crumble before our eyes.

Debbie Blenkinsop from Medical Records put it down to a new understanding of the problems others faced. Taking people around the hospital into areas they had never visited before had opened the eyes of critical medics to the very real problems that other departments faced, and had brought about a profound change of attitude. 'Everybody – doctors and nurses who never understood before – actually went and saw what it was like. Now it's as if we all worked together, and we all came up with the same ideas.' She looked a happier person – for once Medical Records were not getting the blame.

DAY TWO

All through the second day of the workshop the information flooded back into our makeshift training room, and the new procedures for records were worked out. Where ideas could not be implemented immediately, they were put on an action list. Against each action was put the name of the person responsible for carrying it out and a date for implementation, agreed by the person whose job it was to see it done. The final reports were written and the results posted up on highly visible wall charts. I was very pleased that, during the entire exercise, we had never used the concept of blame. We had simply accepted that there must be ways of improving the system. 'Teams,' I said, 'your managers are going to be mightily impressed.'

Michael Emberton and Paul Barrow turned up promptly for the report back, a nice non-verbal signal that they took the whole exercise seriously. They sat in rapt attention as the conclusions and recommendations were spelt out by nurse, doctor and porter alike.

The sorting bag area was to be redesigned, the 'tracer system' amended, the nurses given training in putting the right entry into the computer, the van delivery system improved (without taking on extra staff) and new standard procedures written and constantly updated. Everybody was to be involved in improving the system, and involvement would bring responsibility. No one had any doubt that the records problem could be cracked.

Mark Belham summed up for his group with a rousing declaration: 'With the hope that one day all notes will arrive where they are needed, when they are needed, and we can go on and deliver the service the patients deserve.' (Loud clapping)

To be fair Michael Emberton did not stint his praise. He was absolutely delighted at what had been achieved. This, he assured them, was only the start.

As the teams streamed out of the room, I looked at their faces. They seemed to glow, reflecting pride in what they had achieved. They walked taller, something that always happens when we lift the weight of the dead hand of management off people's backs and exchange condescension for respect.

Michael Emberton spoke to me afterwards of his first impressions. 'We've never spoken to each other before. It's as basic as that.' He was determined to revise his training procedures to replace large meetings at which people are spoken at, into smaller, action-based groups. 'People must feel that when they leave they can go on and achieve something or work at something and then come back and say: "Look at what we've done."'

I was impressed by Michael's embrace of the idea that involvement meant more than being consulted: people need to be involved in the improvement process itself. But the most heart-warming outcome was the new spirit embraced even by the porters, whose jobs were first in the firing line. Brian Farley spoke with feeling: 'If we can do this between twenty of us and radiate out to our different departments the same feeling that was in that room, I think it'll work and I think the management are going to be impressed with us.'

I left Chester that evening hopeful that we had shown enough of the benefits that came from 'peoplology' to make management think again about the sense of contracting out. I was due to come back in ten weeks. Given my initial suspicions of the management style, I still had doubts about whether we could build on this initial success. I needn't have worried.

August brought me back past Chester's familiar town centre and out to the Countess of Chester complex. My first call was at the office of Pat

Smith, in Medical Records. Her face told its own story. After our departure, the Kaizen workshop on records had been continued. One suggestion, deceptively simple, had been to extend an 'amnesty' to anyone sitting on one of the mislaid records. It is a technique used by the police to gather in guns and knives from those who had them at home but didn't want to be incriminated by admitting to it. So why shouldn't it work here in the hospital?

The idea had been a staggering success. 'It's like a little miracle,' said Pat. Eileen Carden of the Records Office filled in the details: 'Ten thousand at least turned up in the first week, and more are still coming in. It was absolutely brilliant. It was something that needed doing and we were really excited about it. Some of these notes hadn't been seen for seven years!'

Where had they come from? Doctors had found them in their filing cabinets and in the glove compartments of their cars, while others had been found on shelves in the wrong department – nobody had seen it as their job to send them back. The important thing was that the records had come back, and patients could now be treated with the benefit of full case history notes.

But while the return of the records was good news what was even better was a dramatic fall in the number being 'mislaid' each week: down from sixty, Pat told me, to twenty. And that wasn't all. The improvement in the internal post service (run by the porters) and the transport service between hospitals had meant that the delays that patients suffered had been substantially reduced.

Tony Duffy, one of the drivers on the workshop, was able to fill in the details. True to the spirit of Kaizen, he had suggested that the labelling on the sorting racks could be redone on the cheap. All that was needed was larger signs with the names of each department made easier to read. But he was delighted when management decided that a good idea was worth spending some money on. 'They just went ahead and wrote a requisition out so we could have it done properly, rather than the Mickey Mouse idea

I had. They've gone the whole hog.' I pointed out that his idea was not 'Mickey Mouse'. While the professional signs had taken four weeks to make, his handwritten ones had been implemented within days.

But had it made any real difference to patient care? Anybody who doubted it had only to talk to Clare Blackwell in the old Royal Chester clinic. She told me that it was not just the booked-in patients who had benefited from the new slick record delivery system. 'The walk-in patients or people brought into casualty at short notice can now have their records brought over because of the extra pick up at accident and emergency.'

More good news at the Medical Records Office. During the workshop somebody had pointed out that an outsider calling into the consultants' secretaries' office with records for Dr Reid, or Dr Mandelson, or whoever, didn't necessarily know who that might be. Chris Mayers pointed out that secretaries were always changing around and a porter would have no idea whose desk was whose. Why not have a sign on the desk that would stop records going to the wrong person to start with? Chris was pleased that the idea had been taken up. But with records still being stored in supermarket-style trolleys rather than in proper racks, he was far from satisfied. 'There's a lot to be done, a lot more to be done.' That's the amazing thing. Once the 'heroes' develop a passion for improvement there's no stopping them... not, at least, in the hands of supportive managers who can see the advantages.

Improvement leads not only to better service – for patients in this case – but also to lower costs. If we remove the fear of being made redundant, the passion for improvement can mean doing voluntarily what a pack of wild horses could not have achieved in the past. Chris Mayers, one of the porters who has most to lose at the hospital, told us: 'Making the records delivery more efficient makes our jobs easier. That means we can do other jobs at the same time instead of wasting time searching for case notes.'

So far so good, then. But as I had stressed again and again to Michael Emberton and Paul Barrow, to keep this sort of cultural change going they needed a new style of management. What they needed was an end to macho command and control, and a switch to supportive, collaborative management that sees the staff as the greatest asset and will fight tooth and nail to protect their long-term interests against some short-term cost-cutter.

I asked Tony Duffy if he had detected a shift in the management approach. He had still to be convinced. 'They've listened in certain areas and made token gestures.' Recently he had been alarmed when he had been asked to vary his run in a way he thought would jeopardize the delivery timetable. 'I refused to do it, and I was told I should do whatever I'm told to do and not question it.' He sighed. 'It just makes you feel you're wasting your time to a certain degree. I thought we were aiming to make things run better and try and smooth the bumps out.'

Some traditional managers might have seen Tony as being awkward, a bit bloody-minded – but this is not how he came across. I felt he really cared about the quality of service he was trying to deliver. Give people some responsibility in managing their own jobs and, as companies have found out all over the world, they can gain a new ally, their own workforce. Tony was in danger of being alienated, crushed before he had a chance to bloom. And Tony was not the only one of the 'heroes' to complain that middle managers were honouring the spirit of Kaizen more in the breach than in the observance. Once I had gone and the TV crew with me, I could imagine that the heroes might soon be nobbled by a few pen-pushers who felt they had to justify their jobs.

So it was a point I tackled head on with Michael Emberton when I called in to discuss how the new way of doing things was going. 'Some of your middle managers, Michael, don't understand what we're doing here. They're still playing the Rambo role. "I tell you what you'll do, and I'll tell you when it's working and when it isn't working, and you'll just do what I tell you." All that sort of crap.' With some discomfort, I thought, he accepted that there was cynicism in these upper echelons. But he assured me there was no cynicism on his part, which I could accept. It was only a start: 'We are only just nibbling at the cherry.'

On the positive side, I found that Paul Barrow had put his personal weight behind a lot of the ideas that the teams had come up with. Perhaps he was not the systems man I had imagined! All that was left was to persuade Michael that he ought to send a letter to Virginia Bottomley, telling her he had found a new way to run his trust. He promised to think about it.

If I came away with reservations about the longer-term prospects at the Countess of Chester, they lay in two areas. First, did Michael and Paul have the bottle to drive through the management revolution? In matters like this, top management has to act decisively if it is to overcome the inertia of the middle ranks, those who feel most threatened by the change. The Samurai warrior had a code which I would recommend to senior executives who set out on this road:

(a) protect and support the weak,
(b) be equal to the strong, and
(c) crush the wicked who would harm my people.

Secondly, I feared that the contracting out would still go ahead. It was government policy, and an NHS trust would find it difficult to resist. But if it was pushed through it could undermine all the progress we had made.

For those of you out there who remained unconvinced, let me leave you with the final thoughts of three of our Chester 'heroes'. If they do not convince you, nothing will.

People can get along together now and thrash things out between them. When we meet again – even in the corridor – we say, 'What about so-and-

so?' Yes, it has helped. It brought us together. We needed to get closer together and work as a team.

Chris Mayers, hospital porter

Our own groups and teams will end today when you've finished. But we say this has got to carry on now, forever.

Janet Capper, secretary

It was very useful to spend time with people that previously you only got to speak to on the phone or saw in passing in the corridor. It was nice to spend that time with them discussing a problem that we all suffer from. It would be nice to think that we continued to have the ear of the management in the future... but time will tell.

Clare Blackwell, nursing sister

Yes, at the Countess of Chester Hospital I found some really safe 'hands' I would be happy to leave the National Health Service in.

Sid, hero hunter

NO MORE CASUALTIES

we will fight them on the beaches
we will fight them in the streets
we will never surrender
...our jobs

it's time
to do it
again!

South Wales was one of the cradles of Britain's first industrial revolution. Under the scenic beauty of the hills and valleys lay some of the richest coalfields in Britain, producing fine anthracite and coking coal. In 1924 there were a quarter of a million men working in the pits. In 1994 there are only a handful of pits and 99 per cent of the jobs have gone.

You can almost feel the air of depression that now afflicts many of the more remote villages in South Wales. The male voice choirs may still sing, and rugby clubs meet in weekly combat, but you can't hide the fact that the stuffing has been knocked out of the community. It is the men who have suffered most. Traditionally here they were the breadwinners, the providers of material wealth. The loss of work has robbed them of their pride, in some cases their very reason for being.

These were my thoughts as I drove down the Tawe Valley to take a look at the last of our six businesses. Of course the mine closure programme has been accelerated by the pursuit of crazy 'free market' policies that operated without regard to communities that depended on such jobs. But in the end the old world was bound to pass away. The real challenge, in areas like this, was to establish new industries and see them grow to provide the new jobs that were needed. As far as the Tawe Valley was concerned, that is not what has happened.

The settlement of Abercraf and Caerbont, 15 miles north-east of Swansea, represents a microcosm of what has gone wrong in the British economy since 1960. The Caerbont factory had its origins as a factory making bicycle chains – the famous Perry chains of late memory. Down the road was a larger factory, owned by Smith Industries and making car instruments, which employed two thousand or so people. This instrument factory fell on hard times when the British motor industry failed to keep pace with its overseas competitors. (We failed to notice the clanking sound as the steamroller caught us up and crushed us!) As a result the workforce was run down and the business sold to Lucas in 1983. Lucas downsized further, closing Smith's London plant and concentrating production in the Tawe Valley. Lucas was regarded as a world-class company, with a tradition of engineering excellence, but the Welsh factory never made a profit. In 1987, after three waves of redundancy which reduced the labour force from 1400 to about 600, Lucas too gave up on motor instruments, and chose to go into partnership with Sumitomo of Japan to make car wiring components instead. The rump of the instrument business moved to the old Perry factory at Caerbont which employed just 200 people.

In 1990 this much shrunken business was sold off to a German instruments company, VDO, one of Europe's biggest components firm. Even German technical ingenuity and management skill failed to turn the business around. In early 1993 it announced that the factory, which now employed only 120 people, was to close.

The announcement was a body blow to the small community in Caerbont and the surrounding villages, following so soon after the closure of the Abernant pit in 1988. Already there were empty cottages all around as people left, taking Norman Tebbit's advice to 'get on your bike'. To make matters worse the only remaining big colliery, the Tower, had at best a limited life. (It was in fact closed in 1994 in the face of protest.)

It is hard for people sitting in Whitehall to appreciate what the steady draining away of jobs does to a community. The Caerbont car instrument factory may have employed only just over a hundred, but the loss of a hundred jobs when men were lying idle at home and young people were leaving school with no jobs to go to was a serious matter. As Jean Nicholas, one of the 'heroes' of the Caerbont workshop, said: 'Young people? Where've they all gone to? They've had to move away. There's nothing else here.'

But the Caerbont factory didn't close. Two unlikely knights in shining armour came riding to the rescue. Peter Catlow, then managing director of ADO UK, but a former senior Lucas manager, had come down to Wales from the Midlands to wind the factory up. He met up with Nigel Bruce, who had worked in the firm since the Lucas days. The two men got on well together and were both convinced that the factory could be made to work. Taking their courage in both hands, they organized an MBO – a management buy-out. It meant mortgaging their houses and raising the balance of the £250,000 needed to buy the company from Investors in Industry, one of the few sources of capital for start-up businesses. ADO (Wales) was reincarnated as Caerbont Automotive Industries, with a short-term guarantee of orders from ADO (Germany) which still had to supply some of their customers with Caerbont-produced instruments. At the change-over, in November 1993, CAI took on about a hundred of the remaining workers, mainly women.

It may have seemed a foolhardy exercise. Two men with limited resources were hoping to succeed where major players like Smith Industries,

Lucas and ADO had given up. But they believed they held an ace that had never been played before. They would use full-blooded Japanese techniques to improve quality and productivity. When he was at Lucas Peter Catlow had been sent to Japan to study their methods. He had become familiar with cellular manufacturing and the principles of just-in-time production. At Lucas the ideas had been put into practice, but he had always felt there was something missing.

At the heart of the Japanese approach, he had come to realize, was an extra ingredient that firms in Britain had not come to grips with. 'To me the biggest lesson of all was the one that says: if you don't use the hearts and minds and talents of your people you are never going to be successful,' he told me when we met.

Nigel was at one with him on this. He had a vision that everyone should warm to, a vision of how the firm could play a role in saving the valley community. 'Our aim is to create a happy contented team that will be here in fifteen years' time, in twenty-five years' time, and so on, for our children's children. Caerbont is not going to disappear, but to grow.'

If I have a mission in life it is to make visions like that a reality. Over the last thirty years British industry has taken too many casualties: three million jobs have disappeared in manufacturing, with terrible effects for communities all over Britain – I think immediately of my own native Armley in Leeds. We have produced a generation of industrial leaders and managers who measure success in 'downsizing' and the bottom line benefits that such butchery brings, instead of improving the existing business and aggressively finding new products and new markets with the confidence that we can supply just what the customer wants. Major Japanese corporations like Mitsubishi manufacture products ranging from giant ships through cars, electrical goods and aircraft to writing materials. But in Europe and America I keep hearing about contracting down to core products and skills. People and their skills are the core of our business, there should be a law against contracting that. As I've said, any fool can make a business profitable by closing down the parts that are losing cash:

those who run businesses need to consider themselves as holding some responsibility for the communities that depend on them. (For those who say, 'Tell that to the shareholders', it is worth pointing out the growing evidence that companies which recognize their wider responsibilities – to customers, to staff, to the local community – deliver a better deal to the shareholder in the long term.)

So Peter and Nigel set about introducing radical Japanese ideas into their business in South Wales, and started to improve it. Why, then, did they feel they needed me to come and run a two-day workshop, and why did I agree to come?

For starters, they had been forced to bring in the changes as a top-down initiative, and, as we know, the history of management behaviour in Britain has often made staff very suspicious of management initiatives. My job was therefore to persuade the staff that it was something they should buy into. But it went deeper than that.

The case of Peter and Nigel illustrates a problem commonly found when companies decide to copy Japanese methods – a problem found as much at Lucas, I guess, as at CAI. We understand the principles behind the Japanese methods, but as Westerners we understand them through our intellects (minds) and not through our emotions (heart). Japanese methods can, in any case, only work if the staff who are going to use them bring to the task their intuitive wisdom, as experts at the jobs they do. Let me illustrate with an example.

Recently a factory I know spent £100,000 on consultancy fees and had manufacturing cells designed and built. The process went something like this. The consultants came in, did a survey and wrote a report – a very thick one, because the company was paying good money for it. The main cost-saving came from making thirty people redundant after the changes were made. (Does this ring a bell?) Then the consultants, mostly young graduates with little practical knowledge of the industry, designed the first cell and had it built.

The cell looks superficially like the ones we built at Rawtenstall, but the differences are profound. Workers in this cell in Wales were given training by the consultants and then tried to work it. Not surprisingly, it didn't work too well. The consultants who had designed the cell had read the books but had no intuitive understanding of the process, and the workers who were now manning it had no sense of ownership. The moral? Cells will only operate well if the people who will work them design it themselves... and they can do.

As far as I could gather, the main problem at CAI derived from this lack of involvement. Though no doubt with the best of intentions, it was still managers and supervisors who had designed and built the cells. So despite all the efforts of Peter and Nigel, the staff still saw it as a management scheme to squeeze more out of them. If the women who worked these cells had been intuitively involved from the word go, they would have owned the process and made a better job of it by continuously improving the way they worked.

people don't resist change
they resist being changed

To be fair to Peter and Nigel, there was also another problem at the factory, associated with its history. These workers had lived with insecurity for years, and insecurity is the biggest enemy of change. According to Peter, 'When we started up, you could cut the atmosphere with a knife. Morale was awful. We had to lose some jobs to keep the ship afloat: understandably the people whom we kept on didn't feel secure.' The result of all this was that the factory was doing well but somehow lacked the 'hearts and minds' commitment that Peter and Nigel saw as essential.

NO MORE CASUALTIES

When I met Peter and Nigel in their office – dressed not in suits but in fashionable Japanese-style workwear just introduced across the company – they told me that they wanted to use the workshop as a launch pad for the battle to win those hearts and minds.

I had no doubt that we could do it. 'You'll be surprised,' I told them, 'at what a difference we can make by applying common sense and restoring respect to people. Once we have switched off that 'beam' at the gate, we'll be away.'

I could see that they were already more than half convinced. Then I waved the can of Bullshit Repellent and made my usual stipulation that there should be no redundacies as a result of my workshop.

They didn't flinch. 'We've already increased employment from about 100 to nearly 140 in just eight months. We intend to grow,' Peter and Nigel assured me.

DAY ONE

The twenty people who gathered together to be given the Sid treatment came from all areas of the factory. As I cast my eyes around the crowded tables in a cramped room, I could see the recent history of the valley sitting before me. Most of the members were women, reflecting the mix among the workforce. Because of high male unemployment in the area – around 25 per cent – many of these women found themselves in the unaccustomed role of breadwinner. Christine Rogers had worked in the instrument plant for thirteen years and seen all the changes. She was married to an ex-miner who had lost his job when Abernant colliery had closed down in 1990. Lorna Thomas, a lively woman with twenty-four years' service, had a husband who was another casualty of the mine closures. Enid Walton, one of the real characters on the workshop, was divorced and had struggled over the years to bring up a son and buy her own house. All of these women worked in the Temperature and Pressure Gauge Department, one of the areas already organized into cells.

Also in their department was Ann Jones, a fine, responsible woman

143

who was shop steward for the engineering and electrical works. I often have union shop stewards on my workshops. They start off suspicious of management motives and full of concern for their members' jobs, as they should be. They can be tough going at first, but once you have won them over they generally become towers of strength, beacons of enthusiasm for the new approach. After all, who will say no to being shown respect and being given responsibility for their own work? Right from the start Ann seemed tuned in to what Peter and Nigel were trying to do.

Taken as a group, the women were a formidable bunch. Outside work they met socially at local bingo sessions or took part in karaoke sessions in the Copper Beech pub in Abercraf.

Among the men (seven out of the twenty) we had a preponderance of supervisors or support workers such as stores and maintenance, reflecting the fact that in this factory men had traditionally held most of the positions of authority. I'll mention three only, because they were to play key roles in the story.

Two of them were identical twins, David and Cerith Close, who had spent all their working lives in the business – over thirty years, going back to the days of Smiths. They were fundamentally nice people but represented part of the problem at CAI. Through David I was introduced to the world of the male voice choir, still a strong tradition in the valley.

The third senior male employee was Roger Morgan, one of the three maintenance engineers, who, as in many British factories, had more work than he could handle. Roger had learnt his craft as an electrician in the local mines and was yet another who had lost his job when Abernant colliery had closed in 1990. He was bitter that good mines had been closed down when they were 'still making a profit'. He had obviously taken a big cut in salary to come to ADO, and that rankled. If Roger had any one quality that made him a difficult member of the workshop it was his belief that he knew it all, and that skilled people like himself could expect to learn very little from semi-skilled operators. His mind was set in the old way of thinking about hierarchies, and nothing was going to change it. (On the seminars I find it is often the 'skilled' people who threaten to stop the creative process in its tracks by adopting negative 'it won't work' attitudes.) Too often this undermines the confidence of the other team members.

To explain this problem, I usually tell my bumble bee story. Several years ago some work was done at the Farnborough Aeronautical Research Centre on the flight characteristics of the bumble bee. Using their computer, one of the most advanced aeronautical simulators in the world, the experts proved that bumble bees cannot fly. If young bumble bees listened to Farnborough experts as they prepared to jump off the edge of their hives, there soon wouldn't be any bumble bees. The moral of the story is this: don't listen to experts who tell you things cannot be done.

However, the problems represented by Roger and the twins were not apparent as I followed my usual pattern, waving the Bullshit Repellent can, discussing the concept of 'experts' and talking about the revival of British industry. As at Stena Sealink, I explained that during the Second World War Britain had been bombed and thousands of people had lost their lives. It was a war that we had won, but we then lost the peace. (You'll recall that since the 1960s our overseas competitors – first the Japanese, the Germans, the Italians and the French, now the Malaysians, the Koreans and the Chinese – had inflicted severe damage to Britain's industrial base, raining cars, fridges, washing machines, televisions, hi-fis and computers on us and destroying not people but jobs.)

What we are going to start today, I said, is a revolution in the workplace which will mean we can hold our heads up again and be proud of our achievements. Most of all, we will take no more casualties. I then explained the difference between the Western and Japanese attitudes to improvement.

In the West we have a 'big leap at a time' mentality, a staircase concept of progress. In this system progress is made in large steps, involving a small team of intellectual experts. While we follow a set of procedures on the factory floor to maintain a standard of quality or a rate of productivity (perhaps using the dreaded BS5750, or even worse, MRP2!), firms spend money researching and developing the next big step forward. When a 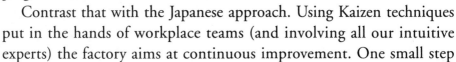 better product or process emerges, the factory gets tooled up with new machines. Suddenly the level of quality and productivity jumps, and this level is maintained until the next great leap forward comes along.

It looks great, but it can't compete with a good Japanese factory. For a start, this stepping up is only a theoretical ideal. As each new level gets established it is normal for slippage to occur, as machines get older or workers (perhaps increasingly bored with the process) become less involved. So the stepping up really ends up looking like this. We are making progress but not as much as we should.

Contrast that with the Japanese approach. Using Kaizen techniques put in the hands of workplace teams (and involving all our intuitive experts) the factory aims at continuous improvement. One small step after another, week after week. Graphically, it looks like a staircase and more like the old-fashioned washing board my mother once used. Because the responsibility for improvement lies with the teams, and because Kaizen allows for constant testing, there's  no slippage. Nobody gets bored when they are involved in making things better. So already the Japanese method delivers a better performance.

But there's a detail I have missed. The Japanese are just as involved in research and development as we are – actually more so. Now do you see why Norton was overtaken by Honda?

'But wait a minute,' someone said. 'The washing board diagram doesn't allow for Japanese machinery getting old and performing less well.' I could only say that the Japanese had discovered years ago that old machinery can be made more and more productive through Kaizen and total productive maintenance (TPM). I had touched on what was to become a big issue later in the workshop.

But before I had gone that far I could feel trouble brewing in the room. We had the usual emotional release of the frustrations that the workers felt: low pay, having to work with old machinery, too much money spent on the office and not enough on the factory, and so on. All this was good healthy stuff – issues which management would have to address. But the real shock came when I developed my theme of continuous improvement (work was to be easier, faster, safer, and fun – 'fun' getting the usual cynical laugh).

I emphasized the advantages that CAI would have over its competitors if instead of four people working on a process we could reduce that number to one. The idea was welcomed like a spoonful of castor oil (remember that stuff?). In front of me were a group of people who had lived through years of decline and repeated redundancies, and I was touching a raw nerve. One person doing the same work as four? Surely that would mean three people getting the sack.

No, no, I said. Those three people would be moved on to other jobs or kept in a paid reserve until new jobs appeared. When Toyota did this, they found that improvements in productivity led to more business. Paradoxically, having fewer people doing the job would make for more orders and more jobs. I then produced the guarantee that Peter Catlow had given on no redundancies.

But, as we had experienced elsewhere, the matter would not go away. There was nothing for it but to ask Peter to come and make the pledge in person, which of course he did. He came over as totally sincere and committed. He communicated not just words but feelings. That did the trick, and we started to make progress. But before we pass on to see what the workshop achieved, it is worth pondering on the lessons I drew from the affair.

In my judgement, Peter and Nigel were two dedicated people who had risked a lot to save the factory. Worker empowerment to them was not just a fashionable phrase to be put in the annual statement, but the key to survival and growth. Already they had increased employment by 30 per cent since taking over just six months previously, despite fierce competition from bigger companies. Many of the workforce expressed admiration for what they had done. When he knew I was coming, Peter had issued a statement about what would be involved in the way of filming and stressed that there would be no redundancies. And yet the message still hadn't got through, or more likely hadn't been believed.

Many managers go out of their way to communicate to the workforce, but there is a vital difference between what a manager says and what the staff hear. Even if the manager is understood at an intellectual level, it may fail to reach the heart. It is essential that our actions send the same message as our words. The whole question of effective communication was to arise later, with the question of dealing with suppliers. For the moment it is enough to let the thought sink in.

but remember actions speak louder than words

DAY TWO

After Peter's personal intervention I felt I had a good three quarters of the workshop people on my side. We could now consider what we might achieve in the one full day that was left.

The workshop was broken down into three teams. The first looked at reorganizing the workplace to make it a nicer and more efficient place to work in. They would start with the Temperature and Pressure Gauge section, which already had cells up and working. As I had walked through earlier I gave it a reasonably high rating as a workplace – what I would have considered a 'good garage'. Their task was to turn it into a 'good kitchen'.

Enid, Lorna, Christine, Catherine and the others descended on the area with piles of pink Post-it notes to begin the clear-out process. Back in the workshop room they planned what they actually needed to work in the area efficiently and where it should go. There was only one obvious problem – Cerith! He was the supervisor, and some of the women clearly found it difficult not to defer to his opinions – and he wasn't slow to give them. Unconsciously he was undermining the dynamics of the whole team. (This is a very common problem if supervisors are allowed to run Kaizen workshops. Supervisors in that position need to be trained to keep their mouths closed and to be supportive, encouraging the flow of ideas from the team.)

I stepped in, placed my hands on his shoulders and said, 'Cerith, you must learn to leave it to the real experts.' His team consisted of women who did the job day in and day out. They knew far better then he did what the job entailed and would come up with much better ideas than he ever could, because in the context of working the cells he was not the expert.

With Cerith suitably restrained, I could sense a surge of energy that was transforming the team before my eyes. Afterwards, on the shop-floor, Enid made it clear that Cerith would be kept on a tight leash. 'We have ways of making people do things,' she said, winking at the camera.

By the end of the session my 'good garage' had become a gleaming kitchen and only the 'tools' that were actually needed to shape the parts were kept on site. They were arranged neatly on a temporary rack. No more time would be lost looking for tools when change-over time came. My biggest concern here was that Cerith would want to reassert his traditional supervisory role as soon as the workshop was over.

LONDON   TOKYO

The second group looked at TPM (total productive maintenance). As at many UK factories, machines at CAI regularly suffered unplanned stoppages during a production run because of breakdown.

'It always puzzles me,' I said, 'that when I fly to Japan, as I'll be doing next month, the plane takes off at Heathrow and lands in Tokyo fourteen hours later. Equivalent to two continuous shifts. What would happen if the jumbo had to come down every few hours to have the engines tweaked to keep them running. That's not funny, is it? If the airlines can do it, why can't we?'

Roger, the maintenance electrician, knew all this already. 'Because the engines are properly maintained,' he piped up. Roger was not the most cheerful of people and he looked pretty bored. There were others in the room who had probably never given the matter a second thought before. They would have benefited from just a little show of enthusiasm.

'So if the planes don't break down when they are properly maintained, what do we need here?'

'A planned maintenance programme!' said Roger with no more gusto.

Roger, I was to find out, had been an advocate of planned down-time for maintenance – just as you would service your car at regular intervals, machines should be serviced too. But he also thought this meant employing more skilled electricians to help him and his fellow maintenance man, Martin. He and Martin were run off their feet, he said. You had to sympathize. But one of the cardinal principles of the Sid Workshop is that all the improvements must be brought in without spending money or taking on more staff. That way there is no need to go through the company for approval of new expenditure.

But this kind of thinking was entirely mystifying to Roger. How could a team of semi-skilled women, working with him, work out ways of creating more time for him to do planned maintenance? As the workshop got down to the task, Roger could barely see the point.

I find people like Roger everywhere. His idea was that the skilled maintenance man (usually a man in the male-oriented world of South Wales) should have a monopoly on maintenance work. In fact, one large part of any TPM programme is to train the operators to look after the machines and to detect early warning signs of something going wrong. Apart from himself and David Close, another supervisor, the team he was going to work with were all female. The women would have ideas on improving maintenance, but would they be allowed to bloom in this environment? I would have to keep an eye on this group.

The third group proved in some ways the most interesting and they certainly opened the eyes of management as to why rejects among components ran very high at 8 per cent. This group was set the task of finding the causes and coming up with solutions. They used a Kaizen chart to do this, identifying faulty types of components, analyzing the nature of the faults and producing solutions. It emerged that most of the problems arose because suppliers were sending parts with holes in the wrong place or of the wrong size. After calling in the purchasing manager, Chris Lynne, they looked at actions that could be taken to deal with the supplier problem. One of the ideas that arose was to send people with actual experience of the problems on the production line to visit the suppliers' factories, rather than leave it to buyers and quality managers to sort it out.

This was great stuff. In the old days companies who suffered quality problems with suppliers would very likely decide to go elsewhere in future, and risk the same problems arising again. But more and more companies are now aware that this is not the answer. It is better to build supportive partnerships with suppliers helping them overcome their problems that in turn are giving you your problem.

But, just as managers can speak to staff without the message getting through, there are, if anything, even more opportunities for lines to get crossed on the inter-company bush telegraph – or, for that matter, inter-company fax. To illustrate the problems let's imagine a salesman who takes an order for a garden swing, and then a factory which tries to make and supply it.

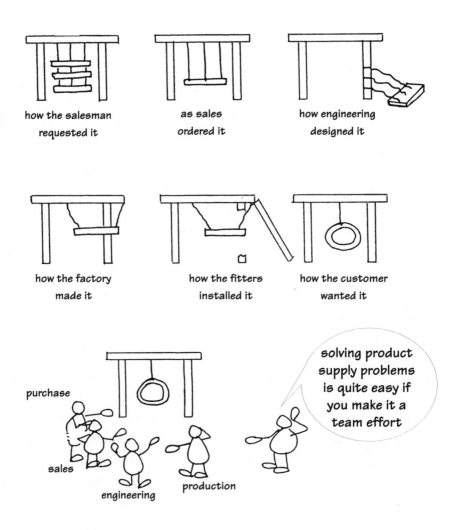

how the salesman requested it

as sales ordered it

how engineering designed it

how the factory made it

how the fitters installed it

how the customer wanted it

purchase

sales

engineering

production

solving product supply problems is quite easy if you make it a team effort

It may be funny, but at the heart of the story there are some fundamental truths. One is: tell me and I'll forget; show me and I may remember; involve me and I'll understand. A second is: like should speak to like (designer to designer, engineer to engineer, assembly worker to assembly worker. The suppliers' experts should talk to the customers' experts).

The CAI idea to send workers to meet their counterparts who worked for the suppliers was straight out of the book of basic common sense. But to make such a plan work to best advantage, companies and suppliers also have to create a common language. Two groups may use English as their basic mode of communication, but it doesn't mean that they share agreement on what even simple words may mean, far less modern business jargon. In this situation, remember my mother's adage that a picture is worth a thousand words. In addition, the Japanese have found that the visual language and conventions of the continuous improvement diagram can create an unambiguous and very focused means of communication. This means that suppliers need to be trained in Kaizen too, which should be the case anyway if they are to flourish and delight their customers.

Customers and suppliers should see themselves as members of a relay team. To win the race against other teams, each member must help his colleague as well as run his own leg. Each member receives the baton from a colleague, and must then pass it on to another. If any one team member fails, it could make the whole team lose.

At four o'clock on Day Two Peter Catlow and his management team ushered themselves in to hear our report. As always, the most striking thing was the transformation of the workshop teams from apathetic 'don't-ask-me-I-only-work-here' types into enthusiastic business improvers. Even the normally glum Roger showed the glint of a smile.

Liz Bennett, a resourceful woman who had been the main breadwinner in her family for years, kicked off with a very professional analysis of what caused the unacceptable level of defects. To drive home the fact that the operators knew all along what the source of the problem was, she explained that she personally had been complaining now for three years about the plastic mouldings that were bought in. 'Provided we take these actions,' she said, referring to the action sheet that formed part of the display, 'we expect defects in components to be reduced in twelve weeks from 8 per cent to 4 per cent of the output, and that's only a beginning.'

Claps and cheers.

Next came Catherine Marsh for the 'Good Housekeeping Team'. Her report included before and after photographs of the Temperature and Pressure Gauge Department. The team had actually chosen to classify the existing set-up as a 'bad garage', showing that they had higher standards than me! As part of this presentation Peter followed the team out on to the factory floor. I noticed with a smile that one of the team, the shop steward Ann Jones, took the Bullshit Repellent can with her, ready to use on the MD if need be. Happily, it remained in her pocket.

Peter was clearly staggered by the change. Although modern, the area had been very cluttered before, with racks of cables getting in the way of production and clogging up the centre of the cells – something that would never have been tolerated in Japan. Now it sported a clear and spotlessly clean face. But, even more interesting were the faces of Enid and the other team members: they beamed with pride. Cerith, who at one stage had said there was no time to make the changes, had clearly been persuaded that he was being unduly pessimistic.

Then Joy Jenkins presented the report of the machinery team. They had carried out an analysis of down-time over the previous twelve weeks and found that it totalled 272 hours. Roger had clearly made a case that the extra production would justify taking on more maintenance engineers! But the team had also looked at proposals for improving maintenance all round, with operators taking more responsibility for their own machines, including resetting the calibration controls themselves. Overall the plan would result in a saving of 50 per cent down-time (and of course without taking on more staff!).

More cheers and clapping.

Peter Catlow, invited to say a few words, announced that he was totally committed to using the talents of the teams as a whole. He remarked that he was amazed that the company had not taken action sooner to make these changes – they seemed so obvious once they had been pointed out. But wasn't that true of most good ideas? However, his most important message was that he accepted the new way of working wholeheartedly (as he always had) and that everybody in the factory must have a chance to learn the Kaizen techniques and be involved in improving the company.

As we packed up to leave it was interesting to hear the comments. Peter Catlow detected a fundamental change in attitudes within the business on everyone's part. Jean Nicholas felt newly motivated to make jobs easier. Cerith Close was impressed by the fact that I was not 'another of these consultants' – that pleased me as much as anything.

Coming back four months later I drove over the moor down into the Tawe Valley with less concern than I had with any other company. Of all the six managements, Peter and Nigel had impressed me most with their sincerity and commitment. In the interim they had asked me to put every area of the company through the same two-day workshop in a crash training programme, even at the expense of losing production on those eight training days.

CAI was on the way to becoming a continuously improving people-based company, sustained by a supportive management style. Only companies of this kind have a long-term prospect of survival in the increasingly competitive world market. And the best can grow and start to turn the tide of manufacturing decline in Britain. No more casualties.

These were my thoughts as I drove up to the CAI factory, now basking in August sunshine. As I walked round the shop-floor plenty of cheery faces turned in greeting. The 'good kitchen' ideal appeared to have spread to the whole factory floor.

In one corner I came across a Kaizen session in operation. Nigel Bruce explained that every team was now to spend one hour a week (called the happy hour) on a continuous improvement session. This was to be no seven-day wonder. As company performance improved, the length of the sessions was to be increased. Standard procedures were under constant revision as these sessions continued. Just as in a Japanese factory the standard procedures were the property of the teams – not of some separate quality or engineering department.

I met Enid Walton who seemed happier. She will never be effusive about work, but she told me that things were 'better'. Certainly, the work area was just as tidy as when we had left it. Jean Nicholas was most excited by the fact that suppliers were now being brought in to sort out the problems. In the office meeting room I encountered one of these new style meetings.

Whereas in the past the supplier had had contact only with the purchasing department, now people were drawn in from all the sections which dealt with that component. Taking a prominent part in the discussion was Liz Bennett, explaining with greater clarity than any buyer could have managed just why the holes had to be where they were. On other occasions teams were to be sent from the factory to visit the supplier's business. Marks and Spencer could not have done it better.

As to the performance of the company, that was on the up and up. In their office Peter and Nigel showed me how production had increased by 250 per cent in just nine months and explained that the rate of increase had accelerated since the workshop, despite the lost production on training days. Waste within the system had fallen dramatically, and quality was on a steady upward trend.

The pair were confident that the gamble they had taken was paying off. 'We're winning new customers and holding on to the ones we already have.' They showed me a customer list that included Volvo, Boss, JCB, Ford and Leyland trucks. But most important of all, they were now making profits that were to be ploughed back into the factory to replace some of the oldest, least reliable machines. (Roger, I thought, would be pleased.) Even the pay gripes were being attended to. They were planning a profit-sharing scheme across the company, the best kind of performance pay available.

Still, not everything had gone perfectly to plan. David Close was finding it difficult to adapt to the new culture and had yet to organize a Kaizen hour for his team. No doubt he felt he couldn't make the time or that it wasn't worth it. Both Peter and Nigel took the view that the traditionalists had to be given time to change, but when the chips were down they would either have to fall into line or go.

In my view there were many fine women already working in the factory who would make ideal supportive supervisors. As so often the workshop and the follow-up showed that women have easier access to the Yin side of their personality (water rather than rock) than men do. But men can learn how to do it.

Then there was the problem of Roger Morgan. He was still resisting the idea that semi-skilled women could do maintenance and wanted the company to spend more money on extra staff and new machinery. He found it hard to accept that even in a people-powered factory there had to be priorities and that spending money in this way was not necessarily the best way to start. The saddest thing for me was that he remained glum and cynical.

But I left Caerbont convinced that this company was building solidly for the future, that one day it could make a significant contribution to rebuilding Britain's strength in an area of manufacturing that, in a moment of collective madness, we allowed to go to the wall. Peter Catlow said the real challenge would be keeping the revolution going once the television cameras had pulled out. He should have no doubts about this.

Once companies start going down this road in earnest there is no turning back – but there's no need to, either. Companies which have harnessed the minds and hearts of their employees to the collective cause have the ability to renew themselves and grow stronger continuously and well into the future. It is not too late for British industrialists to learn that lesson.

As I drove back across the moors I was happy that British manufacturing was alive and well in a South Wales valley.

IT CAN BE LIKE THIS

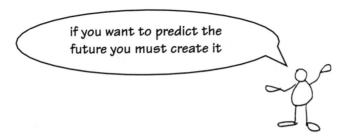

if you want to predict the
future you must create it

Caerbont brought this year's search for 'Sid's heroes' to an end, although I shall continue to release heroes in every corner of Britain as long as there is scope for doing it. Sadly, as things stand there will be no shortage of heroes to be freed from their chains for many years to come.

At least the tide of Western opinion is beginning to flow very strongly the heroes' way. In 1979 one of Japan's leading industrialists, the far-sighted Konoke Matushita, taunted Western businessmen in these terms:

> We are going to win and the industrialized West is going to lose out. There is nothing you can do about it, for the reasons for your failure are within yourselves. For you, the essence of management is getting the ideas out of the *heads* of management into the *hands* of labour [my emphasis]. For us it is the art of mobilizing and putting together the intuitive and intellectual resources of all employees in the service of the firm.

Fifteen years later we are beginning to wake up to the fact that Matushita was making a profound point. Suddenly 'worker empowerment', 'teamwork', 'flat organizations' and 'soft management skills' have become all the rage.

But I have to wonder if we are really taking it seriously, for all the evidence points to Britain being the most backward country in western Europe when it comes to putting ideas of participation and involvement into practice. One damning study early in 1994 came to the conclusion that the attitudes of British workforces were 'the most negative in Europe'. I think the TV series and the six companies we visited show where responsibility for that lies, and how quickly it can be changed.

I find a depressing tendency for board-rooms and senior management to become transfixed, like rabbits in car headlights, by fashionable business jargon, fancy new business ideas, trendy debates on the 'crazy ways for crazy days' and so on. It is all very well reading the latest business classics (something to talk about on the golf course, perhaps) but the litmus test must be whether they lead to action.

In Taoist philosophy there is a very useful concept that I commend: the 'uncarved block'. In the West we take an idea and elaborate on it and discuss it and write about it so much that we can no longer see the simple truth that may lie behind it. This is like taking a block of wood and carving it with exquisite patterns.

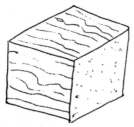

The problem is, of course, that you can no longer see the truth (grain) of the wood. But if we strip the idea down to its essentials, suddenly everything will become clear. Once we have removed the superficial carving from the block the grain is just there, it's obvious.

That is why my system can be reduced to such a few essentials. The guides I give out on the workshops about how to use the continuous improvement diagram, set-up time reduction system and the 5 S housekeeping programme have been reduced to a single A4 sheet (though unfortunately we had to use both sides).

At its heart my system operates on the principle of BCS (Basic Common Sense). If only BCS ruled our businesses rather than BS5750 or ISO 9000! BCS dictates that if you treat people with respect   they will come to treat you with respect (although if you have a group of workers who have been treated as mere 'hands' for years by unthinking managers, respect takes a little while to be earned). This I call the mirror effect: people reflect back to you how you appear to them. Respect breeds mutual trust and a willingness to work together for a common goal. If we can turn this goal into a 'moral cause' so much the better, as Sun T'su recognized 2300 years ago.

But we shouldn't respect people merely as human beings – we should also respect them for the experts they are. In Western society, where intellectual attainment has been raised on an altar and worshipped by the elite, the vast majority of people are made to feel small and insignificant. As a result they are sapped of the energy and enthusiasm which as human beings they all possess. We need to tear down the graven image of 'intellect' and replace it with the wonderful concept of the full, intuitive human being.

Intellectual training has an important place: it can open up the wonders of classical civilization, help us to appreciate

> imagination is more important than knowledge. Albert.

literature and facilitate great technological progress (although great discoveries, strangely enough, are not arrived at by intellectual processes alone – ask Einstein). But what it should not be used for is to try and mastermind complex industrial and business processes. That way lies the calamity brought by the clever consultant!

In any human society, learning through intuitive understanding is much more important than its intellectual equivalent, but because the process cannot be formalized, analyzed or accurately described Western philosophers and scholars have tended to ignore it. Yet how can we have ignored the same processes that have given us the wonder of human language? As children we do not sit down and learn a language through studying grammar and syntax: it comes to us through a natural process of learning not through the conscious mind (children learn the rudiments of language before they have attained the age of reason) but through an unconscious process that we do not properly understand.

Everybody has a store of intuitive knowledge and skill, and it increases all through life – this is the origin of the idea that wisdom comes with age. Once men and women classed by the system as 'ordinary' realize just how 'extraordinary' they all are, we can tap into that pool of wisdom and release the energy and enthusiasm that we all possess. That is why people who have gone through the workshop process begin to see work not as drudgery but as fun.

In the East, philosophers have known this all along. Their world of Zen teaches that too much analysis and conscious thinking gets in the way of the unconscious pool of wisdom. Zhuang Zi, a great Zen philosopher, wrote that just as fish which swim in the ocean do not see the water because it is all around them, we live unwittingly in the realm of Tao. The Eastern philosophers taught that ordinary-mindedness was the way. 'Do not delude yourself by seeking truth elsewhere. It lies within yourself.'

It may sound an alien and strange idea, but in practice it means that inside ourselves, through the intuitive process, is a great reserve of knowledge which can be used to improve our business and private lives. How do we gain access to it? We simply let it flow; we don't think about it – we just do it. The teams who solve the problems in the Sid Workshops do it by letting their thoughts flow freely and scribbling them down on post-it notes as they occur to them. During that process the teams are never judgemental or analytical. Stopping to think simply dams up the flow. But there is more to it than that. Remember the 'hearts' side of the equation. We have got to have the right emotional environment too.

People who feel uptight and anxious will find that their springs of intuitive knowledge and understanding are dammed up.  One way to create the right emotional environment is through the team dynamic of celebration. You must have seen the antics of footballers when one of their side scores a goal: big, grown men hugging each other, all but weeping for joy. Create the right emotional environment and you can release that power in the service of the company. We must let our people celebrate their successes.

This idea of the flow of thought and energy goes well with another strong Zen concept. Think of the flow of thought like the flow of a river. The river can get choked by the growth of weeds – elaborate intellectual ways of looking at things, supplied not by the team members but by intellectually trained managers and supervisors. How often did we see that happening in the course of the TV series! And the flow of positive emotion can just as easily be stopped up by insensitive management, as we saw at Videoprint. A well-known Zen poem explains this beautifully:

A centipede was quite happy until a toad in fun,
Said pray tell me which leg goes
with which?
This worked his mind
to such a pitch,
He lay distracted in a
ditch,
'Thinking' how to run.

The moral of the story is: don't listen to 'toads', just do what you do naturally.

Another feature of water is that it gathers in speed and energy as it

flows downhill. The Zen masters put it like this: Knowledge and understanding are like water that flows downhill; in order to collect the most knowledge and understanding you must be low, not high. By this they meant that humility and respect for others are the first step towards real team wisdom and cooperation.

This image brings me neatly to the question of management style. To bring the best out of the workforce, managers must approach the job from below, not from above. The eastern concepts of Yang and Yin are complementary forces both in the natural world and in the human persona. Yang stands for the familiar masculine qualities of strength, toughness and dominance and is represented by rock. Yin stands for the feminine side: succour and support, the ability to yield, and adaptability. It is represented by water. In the nineteenth century British business was led by tough bosses who would have been proud to be compared to Attila the Hun. They had the qualities of Yang: tough, unyielding and 'bossy' in its original sense. Workers kept their heads down and their shoulders to the wheel. In a market where there was little

competition and products were relatively simple by today's standards, it made for business success.

But the Attila approach won't do for the modern competitive world in which the customer has a choice and companies need to be able to deliver customer delight. As the visits to the six companies should have demonstrated, managers who adopt the macho 'do-what-I-tell-you' policy don't just demotivate the workforce, they stop the flow of ideas that lead to continuous improvement.

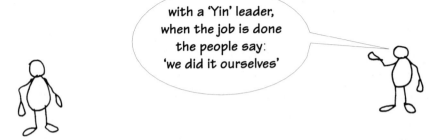

with a 'Yin' leader, when the job is done the people say: 'we did it ourselves'

So what the modern business needs is a manager endowed with the values of Yin. He or she (and women often find it comes more easily) drives for continual improvement, respects people and asks them to do rather than tells them to do, deploying praise and encouragement to help create the right emotional environment. To uncover the truth and to avoid negative emotional states the Yin manager operates a no-blame culture and never reprimands the individual, only the action; this is an important distinction. The Yin-style manager remembers the watchwords: *star managers make their people shine*. And guess what their people pay them back in?

The teams emerging from a Sid Workshop are virtually self-managing on a day-to-day basis. They are given a job to do and they get on and do it. They also assume responsibility for improving the way they do that job, continuously.

This makes the old-style supervisory role virtually redundant. As we saw in the six companies, the supervisors themselves often find the new way of doing things very threatening, and as a result they themselves become the biggest obstacle to change. However, the good news is that many of the supervisors, once won over, become enthusiastic about the new role they have to play. What is that role exactly?

How often have I heard people say: 'Delegation is the sign of a good manager'? It is certainly not that. In fact the middle managers in the empowered business have three jobs: to direct, to motivate and to monitor.

Directing doesn't mean telling people the detail of what to do and how to do it, but setting business targets that have to be reached. All managers have their own elephant-eating job to do, taking the part of the battle-plan assigned to them and breaking it down into manageable chunks for the teams to digest. (Officers in an army have always been trained to do this, because fighting a war is a life-and-death matter. Unfortunately life-and-death struggles in industry are much slower processes, and by the time the people in charge wake up to the need it is often too late!)

When it comes to motivation there is only one important principle to remember: the best fighting troops can only be fully motivated from within. Troops armed with respect and fighting for a moral cause will always defeat an enemy which has no heart for a fight. (Again, some British industrial leaders often fail to learn this lesson until it is too late.) Managers have to learn how to give staff a sense of self-worth and of sharing a common and worthy cause – saving Britain's jobs, Britain's standard of living and Britain's pride. (But no bullshit, mind. The staff will see through any 'con' that would have them give of their best only to be cast off at the first sign of recession.)

Monitoring completes the feedback circle: it informs the strategy and reinforces the motivation. Remember the football analogy. The team members reinforce each other because they all have a common cause/goal and because they always know the score, winning or losing. Companies have to be straight with their staff and keep the information flowing. Secretive management creates suspicion and destroys the common cause.

However, much of the information passing around companies is so dense and indigestible as to induce a bad case of corporate constipation. That's where the Japanese model of simple visual display scores time after time. At Videoprint we saw how a fat manual could be reduced to a few sheets of colour photographs and simple instructions in plain English. In the West, possibly because of our emphasis on 'intellectual' education, we seem over-attached to the written manual and loath to turn to the comic strip approach.

At senior management level the military analogy is, if anything, even more apt. Our industrial general needs to learn from the experience of their best army equivalents. At the top, the need for a strategy and for the correct choice of tactics in conducting the battle against the competition is even more vital.

At Stena Sealink, we saw that sometimes the best strategy is to avoid fighting the enemy on ground of their choosing. The Tunnel could offer greater speed; the ferries should therefore not compete on speed but on offering an all-round holiday experience. However, it would be a poor general who believed that abandoning ground to the enemy is always the best strategy. Sun T'su taught that some territory is just too valuable to surrender, yet since 1960 British industrial generals have done just that. (In the period 1970–90 Japan trebled its production, that of France doubled, while Britain was the only major industrial power to experience no increase at all.) Of course our business leaders have always had excuses for their failures. But when generals consistently lose battles you have got to question their competence.

Of course the casualties have not been the leaders, whose pay packets have swelled, but the ordinary troops who have lost their jobs, and of course society in general. We must not forget that successful economic performance is not just some business ideal, but pays for our children's schools and, directly or indirectly, for our health services and pensions.

By pursuing policies of axing loss-making companies or down-sizing to core businesses, the irony is that we have demotivated and demoralized the very people who once made our country great. The successful Japanese company places the question of job protection at the top of its agenda. The Japanese fight to keep the markets they have (Japan is still big in shipbuilding, despite the rise of low-cost rivals like Korea) and they diversify to exploit new markets. Take Hitachi Zosen, once exclusively a shipbuilding company. Now only 35 per cent of its turnover comes from building ships, while it has diversified successfully into making machinery and even selling tea! By doing so, even though productivity has continued to rise (a situation which usually results in job losses), it has avoided having to make workers redundant.

Some of you will be shaking your heads, mentally crossing swords with the approach. If all countries did that, I can imagine you arguing, then unemployment would have to appear somewhere. Maybe, maybe not. However, the question that should concern us is this: why was it Britain that lost out? We have surrendered too many industries over the last twenty years. Of course, we are now being told that the long retreat is over, that Britain is poised to bounce back as a manufacturing nation. Armed with a very competitive exchange rate, while Japan has to cope with an ever-soaring yen, there is certainly no excuse for not trying. I hope our TV series and this book will help it happen.

But to recover our industrial strength we will have to enlist the full support of the heroes who exist in every factory, office and shop in the country. And, so far, there is little evidence that we have gone any distance down this road. Of the six companies we visited only one, Caerbont, could be safely described as having made real progress in that direction before we arrived. I do not believe, on the basis of my experience, that as many as one in six British companies has made a stab at real empowerment as distinct from the consultant 'bullshit' variety.

Yet the astonishing thing is that through my workshops it is possible to carry through the changes needed in an incredibly short period and produce instantly impressive results. I offer firms their money back if my heroes cannot deliver 'gobsmacking' results within two days, and I have never had to pay back a penny. Before our very eyes, in full view of the television cameras, people have been transformed from hostile or indifferent sets of 'hands' to keen experts adding value to an operation in a way that no computer or robot ever could. People want it to be this way, if only managers could see it. Everybody wants to feel valued and to belong: it is management's stupidity that has deprived them of those basic human needs in the workplace (where, after all, we spend a large part of our lives).

I want to finish with a story and a thought. A few years ago I was invited to watch a championship  Sumo wrestling match in Tokyo. The two wrestlers appeared, one a gigantic man and the other half his size. I thought to myself: 'This won't last long.' And I was right. The smaller man leaped forward, grabbed the giant and bundled him out of the ring. The crowd went mad.

It was only then that I discovered that the smaller man was the champion and that he had done this  sort of thing many times before. What was his secret? My Japanese hosts told me that in Sumo the contestants had the three Ss: strength, skill and spirit. And which do you think was the most important? The story is short. The thought that follows is simple.

Suppose just for one moment that the lessons of Sid's heroes could be applied more widely. We saw in the programmes that when people were shown respect and valued for what they could contribute to the common good they changed from being disheartened and negative people into happy enthusiasts. When you think about it, that is only common sense. People are fundamentally decent – endowed, I believe, with an in-built moral sense. In the work situation, it is only when people suffer from prolonged abuse, albeit often unconscious abuse, at the hands of egotistical managers that they are transformed into bloody-minded members of the awkward squad. (There is much talk in our country about the class system, and how it cannot be changed. Our problem is not so much with class as with people exercising their egos, and that can be changed.)

If this simple truth applies in the workplace, does it not apply equally to society in general? The time is ripe to try injecting a little common respect into our everyday relations, our institutions, our communities. Remember the Samurai code: support the weak, be equal to the strong, crush the wicked. I am not promoting some vision of Heaven on Earth, a modern Utopia. But I don't believe that in reality there are many of us who are wicked by nature. Our behaviour is shaped by our degree of self-respect, our own sense of worth, our tendency to hand out to others the sort of treatment that we ourselves have had to take. Remember the T-junction story; why don't we all start letting each other out?

We could start by making it clear that lack of formal intellectual achievement is nothing to be frowned upon. Let us recognize that intuitive learning is more useful in everyday life, and that all of us have it. To do otherwise is to disable our society. Not only do we lose out because so many people are 'turned off', but when intellect is promoted above intuitive wisdom we can also find ourselves being led by some very clever fools!

In the East the Zen masters believe that too much thought and too much abstract learning only clutters up the mind and gets in the way of Satori or Enlightenment. My mother would have put it differently but just as surely: 'that so-and-so may have brains, but he has no common sense.' It is time for our common-sense people to stand up and be counted.

We started this book with a Chinese proverb, and it is appropriate that we should end with one. It is my favourite, and I think it says it all:

If you want one year of prosperity grow grain.
If you want ten years of prosperity grow trees.
But if you want a hundred years of prosperity grow your people.

the majority of our people have grown. Now it is time to set them free

SOME FINAL THOUGHTS

today is the first day of
the rest of your life

what are you going to
do about it?

We've travelled together through these pages, and I hope you found it an enjoyable experience. You have met some wonderful people, and I hope you will agree with me that the results that my heroes consistently achieve are amazing. But now it's your turn. You can put this book down and carry on as you did before, or you can see it as a starting point for a change in both your working and private lives.

In the pages following these final thoughts, I have suggested some actions you might like to consider. But what I really want everyone to do is release the intuitive 'heroes' that lie within all of us, and start to create that productive pleasant land I spoke of in my initial thoughts. If you are an individual worker you can work with your colleagues to create a workplace where people can enjoy themselves and achieve the amazing productivity improvement you have seen described in these pages. If you are a director or manager you can help your team to create the environment for these actions to take place. You can also protect your team from the 'negative' people who will try to nobble them. The rest is up to you. Speaking as someone who is an expert in releasing heroes, I know you can do it. If you are not sure, please start by using my confidence in you and your fellow workers.

I would like to end this book as I end all my workshops, with my Japanese visit story.

Several years ago the Department of Trade and Industry sponsored a visit to Japan to study Japanese business and production methods. The group visited Nissan, Sony and various other leading companies. Everywhere they went they were welcomed and shown everything they wished to see.

use humility to make them haughty
be extremely mysterious and subtle,
thereby you can be the director of your
opponents' fate   SUN T'SU

At the end of the visit, the group gave a party to thank their Japanese hosts. During the party one of the British visitors asked a Japanese manager, 'Why do you do this? You show us your factories and your production techniques, but aren't you afraid that, with all the money and talent we have in Europe, we will see what you are doing, copy it and beat you?'

The Japanese manager paused for a moment before making this profound reply: 'There are two reasons we are happy to show you. The first is that if you started now it would take you ten years to get where we are today in terms of quality and productivity, and by then we will have moved on.' He then smiled an inscrutable smile and added: 'But the main reason we know it is safe to tell you, is that we know you won't do it.'

He can't talk to us like that! I hope you will agree that our resounding answer must be what we learned from Zen: if you really want to understand the new way, all that remains for you is

JUST DO IT!! JUST DO IT!! JUST DO IT!!

If you're still having doubts, remember what Shakespeare said about them:

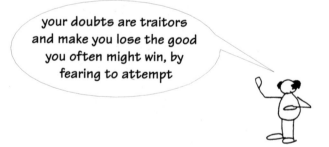

NOW PLEASE, JUST GO DO IT!

ACTION SHEET 1

SUBJECT **Releasing your own 'heroes'**	DATE **Now** LOCATION **Your company**	PRESENT **Directors**

ACTIONS	RESPONSIBILITY	COMPLETION DATE	REMARKS
Meet with your fellow directors and agree if this is the way forward for your company.	You	Set date asap	
Guarantee your people there will be no job losses because of this new way.	You	Set date asap	You need to start a review of your marketing plans. How are you going to turn higher quality – lower costs and faster deliveries into new business. (These are the results your people are going to deliver.)
Put a brief message on all your company notice boards, stating that you want your heroes to join in the running of the business.	You	Set date asap	No bullshit, please. If you don't mean it, don't say it.
Speak to your people and tell them you want this to be the way forward. You must ask for their help in making the new way work.	You	Set date asap	As above.
Identify and eliminate all the 'Mickey Mouse' rules and activities within your company that belittle your people and waste their time.	You	Set date asap	If you don't know what they are, ask your people to write you a list.
Get out of your office and talk to your people.	You	Set date asap	You have some great people out there.
To make sure that everyone in the company understands the message, provide them with their own copy of this book.	You	Set date asap	Contact your local bookseller to order copies.
To ensure that you and your fellow directors have a detailed understanding of your new role, you could attend a TAOZEN management weekend workshop.	You	Set date asap	These are held on two weekends every month. See page 4 for Sid's details.

ACTION SHEET 2

SUBJECT **Releasing your own 'heroes'**	DATE **Now** LOCATION **Your company**	PRESENT **Managers**

ACTIONS	RESPONSIBILITY	COMPLETION DATE	REMARKS
Meet with your own people and discuss how you can introduce the new way of working. Explain that the new rules say: 'Star managers make their people shine.' Ask for their help in making the change.	You	Set date asap	Items for discussion; • Turning the pyramid over. • Keeping in front of the road roller. • Turning the beam off. • Letting people out (T-junction story). • Bringing respect into the company. • Eliminating waste. • Starting and sustaining continuous improvement.
Start monthly reviews with your team in their area, to discuss improvements.	You	Set date asap	Your people need to start measuring quality, cost, delivery and customer delight.
Let your people introduce their own ideas without reference to you.	You	Set date asap	Let them manage themselves as much as possible (they don't have a manager at home).
Praise people when they have done a good job.	You	Now	A simple thank you is always appreciated.
Smile at people.	You	Now	No bullshit. A smile is a form of praise.
Meet with your supervisors/middle managers and explain their new roles.	You	Set date asap	See page 113.
Make sure your team members have their own copy of this book.	You	Set date asap	See your local bookseller.
Start weekly 'Happy Hour' continuous improvement meetings.	You	Set date asap	The continuous improvement diagram is designed to make these meetings a structured, enjoyable and disciplined event. For details see page 187.
To produce the time to do all the above, apply the 50–50 rule to your existing meeting.	You	Set date asap	Reduce the number of meetings by 50 per cent. Reduce the duration of each meeting by 50 per cent. (Now you should have lots of time.)

ACTION SHEET 3

SUBJECT	Creating your new working environment	DATE	Now	PRESENT	Workers
		LOCATION	Your company		

ACTIONS	RESPONSIBILITY	COMPLETION DATE	REMARKS
Meet with your fellow workers and establish how you will start bringing your hearts and brains to work.	You	Set date asap	Items to be discussed • Turning the beam off. • Letting people out (T-junction story). • Bringing respect into the company.
Put up some signs that state what you are really trying to do: That is, to make everyone's job easier, faster, safer and more fun.	You	Set date	Having put up the sign, you must then start doing it.
Start Muda meetings to discuss and eliminate all forms of wastefulness.	You	Set date asap	Remember to involve all your different 'experts' when solving problems that involve several areas.
Set targets for improving QCDD (pronounced Q,C, double D).	You	Set date asap	Your long-term goal is: Quality A– the highest. Cost – the lowest. Delivery – the fastest. Delight – for your customers (and all these measures improving faster than all your competitors).
Choose a section of your work area and transform it from a garage into a kitchen.	You	Set date asap	• Remember kitchens aren't just clean and tidy, but everything in them has a place and that is where it is kept. • Make sure all information on QCDD is displayed graphically in the work area.
Start monthly meetings with your managers to inform them of the progress you are making.	You	Set date asap	Use the charts mentioned above.
Your managers are now working to some new rules that say: 'Star managers make their people shine.' Please help them make the change.	You	Set date asap	Whatever they may have been like in the past, everyone must be given the chance to change.

177

ACTION SHEET 4

SUBJECT **Changing our society**	DATE **Now** LOCATION **Across our country**	PRESENT **Citizens**

ACTIONS	RESPONSIBILITY	COMPLETION DATE	REMARKS
Take the attitude to others you would like them to take to you.	You	Now	Remember life is a mirror.
Start letting people out at T-junctions.	You	Now	Remember the principle: what people receive they will pass on to others.
Stop valuing people by what they possess (style) and value them as a fellow human being (substance).	You		Every member of our society has an important part to play, whatever their position. If we were to compare your dustbin man and the Prime Minister, who would you miss first?
Start smiling more.	You	Now	Smiling and laughter are the antidote to misery.
Every day let us all do two acts of 'random kindness'.	All of us	Now	We can soon get goodness rippling across our land.
Let us all start by trying to be happier.	All of us	Now	It is a lot easier than you think (but you have to understand the rules).

Zen and the art of being happy

happiness is wanting what you have

success is getting what you want

Success rarely makes people happy

to be happy you just have to *want* what you have!

THE TAOZEN SYSTEM -
BASIC TOOLS AND TECHNIQUES

To create a name for this system that creates such 'magic' in our people, I simply combined the two words that have formed a thread through the book. TAO and ZEN. And there it was, the TAOZEN system. I think the name captures the spirit of what we are trying to do.

TAO The flow of events and life, the natural way, constant evolution. Like water, we will always be the correct shape for any situation we are put in.

ZEN To seek enlightenment by personal experience. The only real way to know is to 'do it'.

The key to the success of the workshops, and the essence of the TAOZEN system, is the combination of our heroes' spirit and determination with some very powerful improvement tools.

The Quest for Productivity and Quality

They should not be seen as isolated techniques, but tools to be used for eliminating waste from within the organization. Which tool we use will depend upon the kind of waste we are attacking.

But too often the different forms of waste are hidden under stocks of materials and information. So one of the key improvement activities is to 'walk the job' – go into the workplace and record what is really happening. Then the waste in the system can be clearly seen.

WASTE/MUDA ELIMINATION

The goal is progressively to remove all the activities within your organization that do not contribute to the value of the final product supplied to the customer.

The old economics said:

Cost + Profit = Selling Price

This is no longer true. In our new world the market sets the price and the new economics are:

Selling Price - Cost = Profit

It is the elimination of activities/costs that do not add value (i.e. physically shape the product the customer requires) that is the key to the high profitability of the TAOZEN system. Waste is therefore defined as anything above the absolute minimum of:

Manpower • Machines • Methods • Materials • Minutes

needed to produce the product the customer requires.

Waste can be broken down into eight types (elephant-eating, here we come!).

1. WASTE OF OVER-PRODUCTION

Making more product than the present sales rate. A machine is still producing a batch for one customer (more than he needs), while another waits for the machine to start theirs.

7 pieces made
1 customer has product

customer

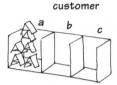

7 pieces made
3 customers have product

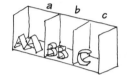

2. WASTE OF WAITING

There can be many different reasons why people and machines have to wait.

breakdowns
changeovers
material
information

3. WASTE OF TRANSPORTATION

Poor layouts and processes can produce unnecessary movements of products, paper and people.

4. WASTE OF THE PROCESS ITSELF

What processes are really necessary to produce the final product? How many others could be eliminated? Bad maintenance of tools and equipment can add 'extra' operations.

5. WASTE OF STOCK

Stock is a waste in itself, but it is also the 'mask' that covers many other forms of waste in the system, and must be systematically reduced to expose them.

6. WASTE OF MOTION

Movement does not necessarily create value added work. Movement of manpower and materials must be minimized.

7. WASTE OF MAKING DEFECTIVE PRODUCTS

Apart from the cost of the defective parts produced, defects will involve all the previous six forms of waste.

8. WASTE OF NOT UTILIZING ALL OUR PEOPLE'S TALENTS

Every individual in the company can contribute 'mentally' and physically to the elimination of waste. To use only a handful of managers and technicians to do the 'thinking' is really the greatest waste of all.

MANUFACTURING AND SERVICE EXCELLENCE – THE TOOLS

A number of tools are needed to help achieve world-class productivity, quality and service.

The programme to achieve this result has three main areas.

JIT	TPM	KAIZEN
JUST-IN-TIME MANUFACTURING	TOTAL PRODUCTIVE MAINTENANCE	CONTINUOUS IMPROVEMENT
Flow of existing and new products through your company	Flow of product through your machinery	Flow of your people's talents and creativity to deliver excellent product and service

1. JUST-IN-TIME MANUFACTURING - THE 'FLOW' OF PRODUCT THROUGH THE COMPANY

For this subject there were two main workshops we used during the filming, which together aim to collapse lead time and inventory. These are:

Cellular manufacturing: Lambert and Howarth

Reducing lead time from days to hours.

A major element of lead time consists of the transportation and storage times involved in traditional batch manufacture.

On this workshop the delegates learned the basic benefits of one piece flow and product based machine groupings. They studied a video of a traditional batch manufacturing shop and then designed a cell using the techniques they had learnt. The goal was to eliminate all unnecessary transportation and storage steps. They then studied the video of the completed cell and saw how this compares with their own solution. They saw a lead time of 42 hours reduced to 17 seconds.

On the second day of the workshop they studied one of their own products and designed and built a manufacturing cell to produce it. The original lead time of 3 weeks was reduced to 48 seconds.

Set-up time reduction: Hotpoint

Reducing change-over time from hours to minutes.

One of the key elements in achieving world-class status is dramatically to reduce lead times and inventories. One of the main barriers to achieving this is the long change-over times on machines.

This workshop was based upon the original work done by Shigeo Shingo at Toyota Motors, and taught its members how to reduce change-overs from hours to minutes. The basic principle is to separate internal steps (work that can only be done with the machine stopped) and external steps (work that can be done when the machine is running, i.e. before or after change-over). Once the internal and external steps are separated, each internal element is studied to find ways of making it easier, which in turn makes it faster. The video case study used illustrated a change-over reduced from 40 minutes to 10 minutes in one day at minimal cost.

On the second day of the workshop the delegates applied the principals they had learnt to one of their change-overs and reduced it by 50 per cent, once again at minimal cost.

Both these workshop techniques must be applied in both production and administrative areas. In the admin. area we treat paperwork as the product.

2. TOTAL PRODUCTIVE MAINTENANCE - THE 'FLOW' OF PRODUCT
THROUGH YOUR MACHINERY: HOTPOINT, VIDEOPRINT AND CAERBONT

Reducing machine down-time and defects to zero.

Fast flow manufacturing and low inventories can become a major liability if machine performance is not reliable in terms of availability and quality.

On this workshop, delegates learned the techniques and team structures required to reduce the major machinery losses to zero, i.e.

1. Down-time.
2. Speed losses
3. Quality losses.

The goal was predictable, consistent machine and production performance using the skills of all the people involved: operators, setters, technicians and supevisors/managers.

5 S WORKPLACE ORGANIZATION	PM ANALYSIS	CREATING A TOTAL MAINTENANCE SYSTEM	AUTONOMOUS MAINTENANCE	POKA-YOKE
Orderliness and cleanliness	Root cause analysis of machinery and quality problems, and their permanent solution	Preventive maintenance, maintenance improvement and maintenance prevention	Operator-based routine maintenance	Mistake-proofing all operations, and ensuring errors don't become defects

These techniques are not normally run as individual workshops but mixed to suit the company's exact requirement.

On Day Two the workshop teams applied the principles they had learnt in their own work area. Typical results were 50 per cent reductions in both down-time and defects. They also transformed an area of the factory from a 'bad garage' into a 'good kitchen'.

3. KAIZEN - THE 'FLOW' OF YOUR PEOPLE'S TALENT AND CREATIVITY:
ALL COMPANIES

Continuous improvement in the workplace.

Kaizen is the key Japanese technique for releasing the talents and creativity of all our people.

The workshop teams were taught the basic improvement techniques for the continuous improvement of productivity, quality, cost, delivery and the elimination of wasteful activities. They learned the team-building and leadership skills that would institutionalize these activities and make them part of everyone's daily routine.

They also learned to use the Continuous Improvement Diagram (see page 187) on a test case example. Again the basic principle is very simple. If we establish all the facts about what is causing a specific problem, and then create an action plan to correct each one of them, the problem will automatically be solved. (The key to success is to have the 'real' experts in the Kaizen team. Then we can be sure we are getting the real facts about the problem, not individuals', opinions.)

On Day Two the teams started a project chosen from their own workplace. Using the Continuous Improvement Diagram, they were then ready to continue running this as their first Kaizen group when they returned to their own workplace.

Total customer delight: Stena Invicta

Making sure we deliver excellent service as well as excellent products.

This workshop involved its members in a detailed analysis of customers' needs and the reason they buy the company's products and services. The teams then discussed the actions that were required to ensure they satisfied the needs of their customers in all their dealings with them.

Establishing the unique activity goals that every member of the service staff must achieve in order to contribute to the overall success of the company is the central theme of this workshop.

At the conclusion of the second day, the team members had a clear picture of the skills and attitudes they must exercise to ensure that their customers agree that it is pleasant and easy to do business with them, and continues to be more pleasant, easier and more profitable than it would be for them to do business with their competitors.

On the *Stena Invicta* workshop, in the four hours teams generated 40 actions to improve customer delight, 32 of which were implemented.

Rules for improvement

1. Respect for every individual team member is the foundation of our Taozen activity. This is why your four main goals are to make everyone's job:
   Easier / Faster / Safer / Fun.

2. Remember - Zen means 'do it'. The only way things are improved is by someone doing something.

3. Your three choices are:
   Eliminate it / Combine it / Simplify it.

4. Ask 'why' five times. Don't accept anything as it is.

5. SOS means:
   Simplify / Organize / Standardize.

6. Define the work that has to be done (work is defined as the motion that produces what the customer requires) and eliminate all motion that does not contribute directly to its achievement.

7. Use ingenuity, not money.

8. Improvement never ends. Wherever you are is where the journey begins.

We already have the 'cures' to all our problems. All we have to do is systematically find them. But how do we find all the 'cures'?

CONCENTRATE on one specific problem, and **COLLECT** all the information we can.

UNDERSTAND the information collected.

RESOLVE the different actions that can be taken.

EXECUTE the actions. **EVALUATE** the results.

SECURE the improvement obtained by **STANDARDIZING** the new procedure, and ensure everyone can see what they have to do.

work to standard / analyze / improve / revize standard

   Make the solution work now and in the future.

Having a standard procedure is not enough. We must ensure everybody works to it.

Working to this system starts and sustains the cycle of never-ending improvement.

Working to standards maintains the system.

187

GLOSSARY OF TERMS

BENCHMARKING
Establishing the best practices of other companies in your own and other industries and using them. (It is always useful to learn from others, but to win you must do things differently from your competitors.)

BCS
Basic common sense, the most powerful improvement tool available to most organizations. What I don't understand is why something so rare is called 'common'.

BS5750/ ISO 9000
A paperwork system (the numbers relate to official British and International Standards, respectively) to record all the procedures to be followed within the organizations. It should in theory ensure that we produce a consistent product, good or bad!

CELLULAR MANUFACTURING
The traditional manufacturing arrangement involves positioning manufacturing machinery and processes of one type in one area. This is called process layout. With cellular manufacturing the machinery and processes are arranged in the sequence required to produce the product - in other words, product layout. This eliminates the transport and storage involved in moving the product from area to area.

CONTINUOUS IMPROVEMENT DIAGRAM
A wall chart and procedure for focusing the talents of a team of experts on any problem and solving it.

5 S HOUSEKEEPING
A procedure for converting any area from a garage into a kitchen.
Seiri Keep in your area only what is needed

Seiton Everything in the area should have its own visually marked place.
Seisou Clean and paint the complete area.
Seiketsu Make it easy to keep things clean.
Shitsuke Have the discipline to follow this system.

JUST-IN-TIME MANUFACTURING
A system developed at Toyota Motors in the 1950s. The goal is to produce what the customer wants, when they want it, in the quantity they want, using the minimum amount of material, machinery, manpower, minutes and money.

KAIZEN
The Japanese word for continuous improvement.

KANBAN
A visual production and product movement control system. In traditional production control, a central planning office controls both assembly and production areas. Product is *pushed* through the system with each area working independently. But with the Kanban system only the assembly is scheduled and when the assembly area requires parts, they send a Kanban card to the production section. These cards are then attached to boxes that contain the parts required. Each card is for a specific part or assembly and specifies the quantity and the type of product the production area should produce for the assemblers. Thus, product is *pulled* through the system.

LEAN PRODUCTION
Another term for just-in-time manufacturing (JIT), or the Toyota production system.

MISSION STATEMENT
In business, a statement of intent. It should be used to define the common purpose of the company and all its people. But too often I find

it is seen as management bullshit and has nothing to do with the majority of the people working in the company.

MUDA

The Japanese word for waste. The elimination of all forms of wastefulness is one of the key activities for any organization.

POKA-YOKE

A system for mistake-proofing our activities (engineering our operations at low cost to ensure our customers cannot receive defective products).

PRODUCT CHOICES

Producing products of the highest quality at the lowest cost, and delivering them faster than your competitors, is no guarantee of your survival. You must also offer your customers a wider choice of product. An excellent example of this is McDonald's, who now serve Mac-chicken, Mac-fish and chips and Mac-breakfast as well as the familiar burgers.

PM (PRODUCT MAINTENANCE) ANALYSIS

A system for analyzing problems, phenomenon and practices involving machinery, materials and methods.

QUALITY CIRCLE

A group of people collected together to solve a quality problem.

STANDARD OPERATING PROCEDURE (SOP)

A set of written and, if possible, pictorial instructions that, when followed, produce a defect-free product exactly to the customer's specification. People who work in kitchens call them recipes.

TAOZEN

A term I use to describe the combination of the Tao (the natural flow of events) and Zen (personal experience - the only way to know is to do it) factors I use in my workshops.

TOTAL PRODUCTIVE MAINTENANCE (TPM)

A series of tools and techniques that are designed to maintain and improve the performance of the equipment and environment within an organization

ZERO DEFECTS

We use the word 'quality' and assume there is an acceptable level of defects. Anyone who uses statistical quality control techniques can even tell you what they are. But we must always remember that the customer never wanted us to send them any defects. Zero defects is our ultimate goal. (See Poka-Yoke.)

FURTHER READING

Remember, reading books alone will not teach you how to do things - you will only succeed by actually doing something.

Hoff Benjamin, *The Tao of Pooh* - Mandarin, 1990
Kaing Koh Kok (translator), *The Book of Zen* - AsiaPak Comic Series, 1992
Roddick Anita, *Body and Soul* - Vermilion, 1992
Shingo Shigeo, *A Study of the Toyota Production System* - Productivity Press, 1989
T'su Sun, *The Art of War* - AsiaPak Comic Series, 1991

INDEX